Sermon on the Mount

BLESSINGS *of* THE
KINGDOM

Lifeway Press®
Brentwood, Tennessee

ISBN: 978-1-0877-8366-6 • Item: 005842155

Subject Area: Bible Studies, Dewey Decimal Classification Number: 226.9
Subject Heading:Bible Gospels and Acts—Sermon on the Mount—Study and Teaching/ Christian Life
Printed in the United States of America

Lifeway Christian Resources, 200 Powell Place, Suite 100, Brentwood, TN 37027-7707.

We believe that the Bible has God for its author; salvation for its end; and truth, without any mixture of error, for its matter and that all Scripture is totally true and trustworthy. To review Lifeway's doctrinal guidelines, please visit www.lifeway.com/doctrinalguideline.

CONTENTS

INTRODUCTION

When a rock band or popular singer has been successful and around for a while, they eventually produce a "Greatest Hits" album—a collection of their most influential and famous songs taken from their whole catalogue of tunes. Today if you search for an artist through Apple Music or Spotify you'll find "Taylor Swift: Essentials" or a playlist entitled "This is Eagles" where some expert has curated for us a group of the musicians' most representative songs.

When we turn to the New Testament, we find several God-inspired artists telling us about who Jesus is and why He matters to our lives. One of the most influential of these artists is Matthew, whose biography about Jesus stands at the head of the New Testament: The Gospel of Matthew.

Extending our musical analogy, Matthew has curated for us some of the "greatest hits" of Jesus's teachings, all for the purpose of shaping us as followers of Christ. Matthew's "Jesus: Essentials" playlist is structured around five blocks of teaching (Matthew chapters 5–7; 10; 13; 18; 23–25). And the most famous of these famous songs—the "Hotel California" (the Eagles) or "All Too Well" (Taylor Swift) song within the Greatest Hits album—is the first teaching block, what we call the Sermon on the Mount.

At least since the time of Augustine, Matthew chapters 5–7 has been given the name "Sermon on the Mount" because of its symbolic mountaintop location. Like many pastors and theologians from the early days of the church down to today, Augustine wrote a whole commentary just on these three chapters of Matthew. This is because within these chapters of Jesus's teaching we have some of the most powerful images and pointed exhortations found anywhere in Scripture. The Sermon on the Mount contains many of Jesus's most memorable sayings such as "blessed are the poor in spirit," "turn the other cheek," "don't judge lest you be judged," and "do to others as you would have them do to you." As a result, Matthew 5–7 has been one of the most studied, written about, and preached upon portion of the Bible throughout the church's history.

The Gospel of Matthew: Purpose and Structure

Before we turn to our study of the Sermon it will be helpful to make sure we understand a little bit about the Gospel of Matthew overall because the Sermon cannot be interpreted well apart from the broader story of which it is a part.

Our Gospels are simultaneously **historical, theological, and forma-tive**. All three of these descriptors are important. They are teaching us what really happened during Jesus's life (**historical**) because Christianity is not just a set of mythological ideals divorced from real historical events. But history telling is not all the Gospels are doing. More than being a mere record of what happened, the Gospels are intentionally teaching us how to understand who God is as revealed through Jesus (**theological**). As a result we are also being invited to learn to inhabit the world in Jesus's ways and to become different people, disciples of Jesus (**formative**). As we go through this study we will see that the theological and formative aspects of the Gospels are particularly important for a good interpretation of the Sermon.

Our four Gospels all work together in four-part harmony to tell us about the life, death, and resurrection of Jesus. They are all singing the same song but do so in different ways. Matthew is particularly interested in showing us how Jesus is the end point or goal of all that God has been doing since the creation of the world. The biblical word Matthew uses to sum up this truth is *fulfillment*. Jesus brings to completion and shows the true meaning of all the events, people, institutions, and truths of Israel's history. Once again, understanding this will be crucial in interpreting the Sermon well.

In the ancient Greco-Roman world people often wrote biographies of important military, political, and philosophical leaders. Our four Gospels fall into this same category, except with the added claim that Jesus is God Himself and is now risen from the dead, calling all people to believe in Him and become disciples. An ancient biography provided two things that were important—a record of what the person said (his or her teachings) and what the person did (his or her model of life). This combination of word and deed is exactly what we find in the Gospels. Matthew gives us a large collection of stories of the things Jesus did and said.

Students of Matthew have long observed that Matthew provides five big blocks of Jesus's teachings (**called the Five Major Discourses**) that are woven into his narrative. These teaching blocks are thematic, that is, they are teachings that center around a certain big idea that Jesus wants to communicate. The structure of his Gospel account looks like this:

- The Introduction of Jesus's Ministry and Mission (1:1–4:25)
- First Teaching Block—the Sermon on the Mount (5:1–7:29)
- Stories of Jesus's Ministry (8:1–9:38)
- Second Teaching Block—Instructions to His Disciples (10:1–11:1)
- Stories of Opposition to Jesus (11:2–12:50)
- Third Teaching Block—Parables About the Kingdom of Heaven (13:1-53)
- Stories of Jesus Creating a New People of God (13:54–17:27)
- Fourth Teaching Block—Life Together for the People of God (18:1–19:1)
- Stories of Jesus and His Disciples in Conflict (19:2–22:46)
- Fifth Teaching Block—Judgment Now and in the Future (23:1–25:46)
- The End of Jesus's Earthly Ministry and the Completion of His Mission (26:1–28:20)

While our focus in this study will be on that first teaching block, it is helpful to see that this is not all that Jesus taught or did in Matthew's Gospel. We cannot isolate the Sermon from the rest of what Matthew is teaching us about Jesus. When we study the Sermon we should regularly seek connections between what we find there and the rest of Matthew's Gospel.

The Sermon on the Mount as a Vision for Life

As noted above, each of Jesus's teaching blocks is centered around a big idea, a theme that is the focus. **What theme or idea is central to the Sermon?** To answer this we can first observe that the Sermon is not a haphazard collection of sayings but is structured very intentionally around a series of triads that can be outlined like this:

ASCENDING AND SITTING (5:1-2)

A. Introduction: The Call to God's People (5:3-16)

1. Nine Beatitudes for the New People of God (5:3-12)

2. The New Covenant Witness of the People of God (5:13-16)

B. The Body: The Greater Righteousness for God's People (5:17–7:12)

1. Greater Righteousness in Relation to God's Laws (5:17-48)

   a. Proposition (5:17-20)

   b. Six Exegeses/Examples (5:21-47)

   c. Summary (5:48)

2. Greater Righteousness in Relation to Piety toward God (6:1-21)

   a. Introduction: Pleasing the Father in Heaven, not Humans (6:1)

   b. Three Examples (6:2-18)

   ** Central Teaching on Prayer (6:7-15)

   c. Conclusion: Rewards in Heaven, not on Earth (6:19-21)

3. Greater Righteousness in Relation to the World (6:19–7:12)

   a. Introduction (6:19-21)

   b. In Relation to the Goods of This World (6:22-34)

   c. In Relation to the People of This World (7:1-6)

   d. Conclusion (7:7-12)

C. Conclusion: Three Warnings Regarding the Prospect of Eschatological Judgment (7:13-27)

1. Two Kinds of Paths (7:13-14)

2. Two Kinds of Prophets (7:15-23)

3. Two Kinds of Builders (7:24-27)

DESCENDING AND ACTION (7:28–8:1)

There is a clear structure to Jesus's teaching here. The main point is found in Matthew 5:17-20—that Jesus did not come into the world to abolish or ignore what God has said or done in the past. Instead, Jesus says, He has come to "fulfill all righteousness" (3:15). In this first collection of Jesus's teachings, He is explaining what this true fulfilled righteousness looks like, that is, what it looks like to live as God's creatures, made in His image, under His gracious reign with Christ as King. The Sermon on the Mount paints a picture of what this way of greater righteousness looks like in our lives in very practical ways—in relationship to God, to others, and to the world (5:21–7:12).

This overall theme of true righteousness is introduced with Jesus's famous Beatitudes (5:3-12) because this is the end goal of Jesus's teachings—that we find true life, *shalom*, happiness (in the biblical sense). The Sermon ends with a threefold exhortation to learn from Jesus and thus grow in godly wisdom (7:13-27). In the middle of this is Jesus's focused teaching on the question of what true righteousness looks like.

And the answer to this question is that true righteousness requires wholeness (5:48; Greek, *teleios*). **Wholeness means that our external actions match our internal dispositions, that our lives align with our hearts, and vice versa.** When we have hearts that are supposedly oriented to God but lack expression in what we actually do, we are like fruitless trees (7:15-20).

On the other side, if we have actions that look good but lack hearts that truly love God and others, then we are hypocrites (6:1-2; see also 23:1-36). The solution to both of these false forms of righteousness is becoming whole, growing in maturity so that over time our heads, hearts, and hands all operate in unity. This unity is what ancient people called virtue or practiced wisdom (7:24).

As we study the Sermon we will see this idea repeated throughout the wonderfully crafted structure of the message. Jesus's point is not to condemn us but to invite us to find life and life in abundance (to use Jesus's language from John 10:10). Jesus is providing the true vision for life as God's creatures who have been invited into His kingdom, a kingdom that is here in Jesus now and will become fully so at Jesus's second coming into the world at the end of the present era.

Jesus's Invitation

All this talk of necessary righteousness could be wrongly interpreted as a burden or something crushing to our souls. Some people might think this sounds like the opposite of grace, but it is not. Jesus is calling us to become whole-person disciples, to have lives that are increasingly marked by righteous living, but this is not a duty or new law, but an invitation to what every human being was made for and longs for: true flourishing that can be found only in relationship with God.

In Matthew 11:25-27 Jesus boldly claims that knowledge of God only comes through knowledge of Himself, which itself comes only through the gift of revelation. He goes on to speak these famous words—"Come to me, all of you who are weary and burdened, and I will give you rest. Take up my yoke and learn from me, because I am lowly and humble in heart, and you will find rest for your souls. For my yoke is easy and my burden is light" (11:28-30).

Herein we see the proper way to understand Jesus's call to be disciples, to walk in His narrow way (7:13-14), using the metaphor of an oxen yoke. To be a disciple is to take upon our necks and shoulders a constraining burden, bending our wills to someone else's to be guided. Rather than being negative and crushing, we experience the beautiful paradox of God's ways— freedom comes through submission, life comes through death, *shalom* comes through a yoke. This is because Jesus's yoke actually gives us life. He is inviting us by faith to trust that following Him will grant us true life in God's kingdom. The Sermon on the Mount is one of Jesus's explanations and applications of this life-through-yoke principle. Through studying and being transformed by the Sermon we will enter God's gracious kingdom through Christ.

1

JESUS'S (SHOCKING) VISION FOR THE TRULY BLESSED LIFE

MATTHEW 5:1-16

Pop quiz: What do all people at all times want? Is there anything that we can identify as universal and timeless that drives how all humans live? If so, what is it?

That question is not new. It's been asked and answered for as long as people have been wrestling with what it means to be human. In the Greco-Roman world, before and during the time of Jesus, this question was discussed often by the great philosophers. The answer they gave was consistent. Likewise, in the first eighteen hundred years of the church this question was asked by theologians and, maybe shockingly to us, they gave the same answer. All people want to be happy.

Let's listen to what the influential church leader Augustine had to say on the issue. In Book 10 of his massive tome *The City of God*, he begins this way: "It is the decided opinion of all who use their brains, that all men desire to be happy."[1]

Happiness—a sense of peace, thriving, and contentment, not just a temporary pleasure—drives all that we do. It is fundamental to what it means to be human. We are creatures made in God's image and we are designed for flourishing—what the Bible calls *shalom*. In this assessment, Augustine agrees with all the philosophers and theologians that came before him.

We are no different today. Standing in line at my neighborhood Lowe's to buy some deck-building materials, I spied a magazine entitled, *The Happiness Formula: How to Find Joy & Live Your Best Life*. It contained a glossy ninety-five pages of essays, pro tips, charts, and graphs about the "science of happiness." In short, snappy articles, we are told how "modern science," by which they mean positive psychology, teaches us what to do and not do to be happy. Eat right. Avoid bad relationships. Ride bicycles more like the happy Swedish people do. Practice yoga. Even a home improvement store is offering help on the happiness question.

But what about the Bible? And what about Jesus? Doesn't He teach us to deny ourselves and take up our crosses (Mark 8:34)? Yes. Isn't this the opposite of our desire for happiness? No.

Quite the contrary, Jesus's call to become His disciples, which includes suffering and self-denial, is never an end in itself. Jesus's call is an invitation to find true *shalom*. **According to Jesus, the goal of cross-bearing and self-denial is so that we might find the flourishing life (true happiness) that we are made for.** As Jesus says elsewhere, He came into the world not to condemn us or to give us a new set of duties, but so that we might find abundant life (John 10:10).

This is the drive for ultimate happiness that Augustine was talking about, and it's found all over the Bible. God is constantly appealing to us to turn to Him and live in His ways because He loves us as His children and creatures. He knows we will only find true life as we live according to His ways.

There is no place where this is clearer than in the opening section of Jesus's famous Sermon on the Mount. We call Jesus's first teaching the Beatitudes (Matthew 5:3-12) because the Latin word *beatus* means "happy" or "flourishing." (See Closer Look.) Jesus opened His most famous sermon with nine declarations or "macarisms" about where to find true happiness. We'll see how He defined happiness is not what we expect. But like all philosophers and theologians, He's addressing the same question—*How do we find true happiness?*

As we turn to study the Beatitudes, it is good to recall how the whole Sermon is structured. Matthew 5:17-20 contains the central idea—Jesus is teaching us how to live in God's ways (being "righteous") through becoming whole people. Matthew 5:1-16 is the introduction to this teaching that appeals to our most basic human desire—to find true life.

In this introduction to the Sermon, Jesus explains in shocking ways where true life is to be found—through following His model of humility and even suffering (5:1-12). He will then invite His disciples to be His priests in the world, proclaiming and living out this same message (5:13-16).

A CLOSER LOOK

Makarios

Most English Bibles use the word *blessed* to translate Jesus's nine Beatitudes. The concept of "blessing" is an important one in the Bible and so this is an understandable translation. However, in English, *blessed* is ambiguous. We can use the English word *bless* to refer to God actively creating life and flourishing for us (the act of blessing) but we can also use it to describe the state of someone who is flourishing (the state of true happiness or *shalom*).

Hebrew, Greek, Latin (and most other languages) have two different words to describe these two different senses of *bless* but English does not. And this is where the problem lies. The Greek word used in the Beatitudes is *makarios*, which communicates the state of someone who is experiencing true happiness or flourishing. This is the same word used many places in the Old and New Testaments, including in Psalm 1, which has many parallels with the Sermon. This is not the word used to describe God actively blessing someone. Rather, *makarios* (Hebrew, *asher*; Latin, *beatus*) is used when a sage is explaining to his disciples the way to live that will bring true life. *Makarios* is the word used when a father or mother speaks proverbial wisdom to his or her children in hopes that they will find a good life. These kind of wisdom statements are called *macarisms* or *beatitudes*. This is what Jesus the Sage is providing here—the true vision of how to inhabit the world that aligns with God's coming kingdom, the only way we humans can find true life.

Unfortunately, due to our confusion over the word *blessed*, many misunderstand Jesus's Beatitudes as if they are commands to live a certain way or promises of God's blessing. This misunderstands what a macarism is. Jesus is not demanding nor cajoling us to be humble or merciful so that we will get God's favor. Rather, as God's Wisdom incarnate He is casting a vision for how to orient our hearts and lives, following His own model, so that we can find the life we are made for.

Jesus the Sage
MATTHEW 5:1-2

It would be easy to overlook these short opening words, but we would miss some important truths. Matthew tells us Jesus began His teaching ministry by ascending a mountain and sitting down. In the hilly terrain of Israel, an elevated place provided a good natural auditorium for the growing crowds following Jesus. But there was something more significant going on than this.

In every religion, mountains or "high places" are important because they are seen as places of revelation, of seeing—not only physically but spiritually. This was certainly true in Israel's history as well, with many key moments occurring on mountains, such as at Mount Ararat, Mount Carmel, Mount Gilead, and others. **Mountains will also play an important part in the rest of Matthew's story about Jesus** (15:29; 17:1-13; 24:1–25:46; 28:16-20).

But the most significant connection being made between Jesus and Israel's history is the comparison with Moses on Mount Sinai (Exodus 19:3; 24:15-18; 34:1-4). Throughout the preceding four chapters, Matthew made several allusions to connect Jesus with Moses. Israel's great moment of deliverance from Egypt that led to God revealing His covenantal instructions (Torah, Law) to His people is being recalled and surpassed by Jesus. Jesus is presented as the fulfillment of all that God has done in the past—affirming, completing, and transforming God's revelation for the final era of history. Even as the old covenant was given through Moses on Mount Sinai, now the new and better covenant is manifested on the Mount of the Beatitudes through the One greater than Moses (see John 1:1-18).

Matthew tells us that Jesus sat down. Once again, this is not merely a historical or physical reference, but communicates something deeper: Jesus is shown as authoritative. Teachers, philosophers, and judges in the ancient world often sat down while their hearers gathered around. This communicated respected authority, with the "chair" becoming a symbol of such teaching. Later in Matthew, Jesus will refer to the scribes and Pharisees as "seated in the chair of Moses" (Matthew 23:2), which is itself a reference to Moses sitting as judge/interpreter in Exodus 18:13. In the Roman Catholic tradition, the same idea continues with authoritative religious and legal matters coming from the Pope described as *ex cathedra* ("from the chair"). This is how Jesus is presented—as seated with authority on a mountain.

These introductory two verses set us up to listen carefully to the words of authoritative divine revelation about to flow out of Jesus's mouth.

View of the Sea of Galilee from
the Mount of Beatitudes,
Sea of Galilee, Israel.
ILLUSTRATOR PHOTO/G.B. HOWELL

Friends in High Places

Mountains are significant geography in the Bible, often serving as the setting for amazing to history-changing events. Read the Scripture references to answer the questions below.

1. After the earth was flooded, Noah's ark came to rest at Mount Ararat (Genesis 8). This important saga contain a vital promise that God would not flood the earth again. What was the important symbol?

2. Abraham climbed Mount Moriah with his son Isaac to sacrifice him—but God provided an alternative (Genesis 22). What was it? What did it symbolize?

3. Mount Sinai was the site of two significant experiences for Moses with two very striking reminders of God, the burning bush and the Ten Commandments. After receiving the Ten Commandments, Moses found the Israelites worshiping a symbol of paganism (Exodus 19–20). What was it?

4. Elijah defeated the prophets of Baal on Mount Carmel (1 Kings 18:16-46). What was the symbol of power he employed?

5. Later Jesus ascended to heaven from the Mount of Olives (Acts 1:9-12). Who were the men in white standing there? Who or what do you think they intended to symbolize?

Based on this sample of passages—and there are more—what would you say a mountain symbolizes in the Bible? Read Psalm 121:1 for inspiration.

How does that compare with the other symbols depicting sin?

The Happy Life in Relationship to God
MATTHEW 5:3-6

As noted above, Jesus began His authoritative teaching with nine Beatitudes or macarisms. These are nine answers to the great question, *How do we find the truly flourishing life?* Together these Beatitudes create an overall vision for what it means to live as God's people. As such, **they should be taken together as a whole, not just individually.** They provide a composite picture of the life of God-centered wisdom.

At the same time, these statements of happiness are not meant to be comprehensive; they're not the only thing the Bible says about finding true life. Nor should we read these Beatitudes expecting them to give us a to-do list that we are to dutifully check off (as if that were possible anyways; have you read the list?). Rather, Jesus paints a picture of what a kingdom disciple looks like in terms of heart-posture, habits, sensitivities, and attitudes.

We should also note how Jesus's Beatitudes are kingdom oriented. The first and eighth Beatitudes are framed with the phrase, "For the kingdom of heaven is theirs" (5:3,10), emphasizing the theme of God's kingdom that glues it all together. Matthew has already made it clear in the preceding chapters that Jesus's message is about God's kingdom of heaven coming to earth through Jesus (see later Jesus's instruction to pray specifically for this in 6:9-10). This message was what John the Baptist preached (3:2) and is also the summary of Jesus's announcement (4:17)—"Repent, because the kingdom of heaven has come near." Now in the Beatitudes, Jesus makes clear who is in God's kingdom and who is not—those whose lives bear the fruit of what the Beatitudes depict.

When we take the Beatitudes as a whole, we see they can be grouped in a number of ways. For our exploration we will examine the Beatitudes in 4-5 pattern.

> *Blessed are the poor in spirit,*
> *for the kingdom of heaven is theirs.*
> *Blessed are those who mourn,*
> *for they will be comforted.*
> *Blessed are the humble,*
> *for they will inherit the earth.*
> *Blessed are those who hunger and thirst for righteousness,*
> *for they will be filled.*
> **MATTHEW 5:3-6**

In this first grouping Jesus describes a kingdom disciple as one whose life is distinguished by a posture of **great humility, brokenness, and dependence on God** (5:3-5). This can be summed up as "hungering and thirsting for righteousness" (5:6).

"Poor in spirit" (5:3) uses the metaphor of poverty to describe the person who rightly sees himself as destitute before God, having no claim or power, but casting himself upon God's kind mercy.

"Mourning" (5:4) can refer generally to one's experience of grief and loss in this broken world. More specifically this also speaks to how the believer in God feels about one's sins, alluding to the great words of Isaiah 40:

> *"Comfort, comfort my people,"*
> *says your God.*
> *"Speak tenderly to Jerusalem,*
> *and announce to her*
> *that her time of hard service is over,*
> *her iniquity has been pardoned,*
> *and she has received from the LORD's hand*
> *double for all her sins."*
>
> **ISAIAH 40:1-2**

These words are part of the great promise that God is going to send the Messiah who will restore God's kingdom and people on the earth (see the following verses in Isaiah 40:3-11 which are quoted in the New Testament).

In the third macarism, Jesus states plainly that the "blessed" (truly happy) ones are humble, recalling the consistent teaching in both testaments that God is opposed to the proud but resides with and exalts the humble (Isaiah 2:12; Psalm 31:23; Psalm 138:6; Proverbs 8:13; James 4:6; 1 Peter 5:5).

The fourth Beatitude concludes this first section by describing disciples as ones who **"hunger and thirst for righteousness"** (5:6). This can be read as a summary statement for how we are to live as Jesus's disciples in the world—looking to God, longing for Him to return and restore His good reign upon the earth. This is the normal sense of "righteousness" in the Bible—things being done rightly according to God's revelation. To hunger and thirst for righteousness means that we see the injustice, brokenness, and pain of this world and because our hearts are attuned to God we experience pangs of hunger and thirst. This is how Jesus will teach us to pray in the Lord's Prayer (Matthew 6:9-15)—that the heavenly reality of God reigning fully will become our experience on earth as well.

As with all of Jesus's Beatitudes, He not only offers the statement of what the *shalom* life looks like, but He also provides a corresponding reason in the second half of the saying why His statement is true. He not only declares the goodness of poverty of spirit but also explains that this posture is accompanied by a further blessing from God, "For the kingdom of heaven is theirs." So too, the mourners will be comforted and the humble will inherit the earth. Those hungering for God's righteousness to be restored on the earth will have their mouths filled.

Be Attitudes

The Beatitudes present a compelling picture of what it means to thrive as a Christian. Identify these biblical examples of human beings living in a state of blessing:

Impoverished_____: Acts 3:6

Mournful _____: Luke 7:36-50

Humble_____: 1 Timothy 1:15

Hungry and thirsty_____: Luke 10:38-42

With which person do you most identify?

While these stories depict living examples of each of the Beatitudes, keep in mind Jesus shared the Beatitudes as a composite picture and we can also assume that these followers of Christ were well-rounded, displaying not just one of these traits but all of them, at least some of the time.

Which example challenges you the most?

These follow-up statements are the explanation for why the crazy-sounding definition of happiness Jesus just gave actually makes sense from a divine perspective. While Jesus's explanation of true happiness is not at all what we would expect (or initially desire), we can embrace His paradoxical way of living with the faith that God will be present with us and meet our desires and needs even in the midst of our humble state.

The Happy Life in Relationship to Others
MATTHEW 5:7-12

In this second half of the Beatitudes, **Jesus shifts from our posture toward God to our attitude and habits toward our fellow humans.** This is a typical pairing throughout the Bible, as in the two parts of the Ten Commandments (Exodus 20:1-17) and in the first and second greatest commandments (Matthew 22:34-40). We are fundamentally relational beings, so we need to learn to relate in life-giving ways to both our Creator and fellow creatures.

> *Blessed are the merciful,*
> *for they will be shown mercy.*
> *Blessed are the pure in heart,*
> *for they will see God.*
> *Blessed are the peacemakers,*
> *for they will be called sons of God.*
> **MATTHEW 5:7-9**

The first three Beatitudes in this section invite us to find true happiness by living in relationships of mercy, love, and forgiveness toward others. This is seen most clearly in verses 7 and 9. Jesus tells us when our lives are marked by being merciful, we will experience mercy from God as well as others. This circle of mercy giving and receiving creates a thick web of meaningful relationships and thereby goodness in life. Likewise, being a peacemaker does not refer in the abstract to pacifism or world peace, as beneficial as these things might be at times. Being a peacemaker speaks to how we habitually relate to others, especially when conflicts, hurts, and tensions arise. Christ's disciples are the ones who seek reconciliation, making peace rather than bringing heat and anger to moments of interpersonal skirmishes.

This theme of mercy and peacemaking can be found both deep and wide in Jesus's teachings in Matthew. Indeed, in Matthew the primary moral characteristic that Jesus calls His disciples to embody is found in an overlapping cluster of ideas—mercy, compassion, and forgiveness. Mercy is a rich idea biblically that has two sides in Matthew—mercy as compassion on those in need and who are suffering (regardless of whether this is their own fault or not) and mercy as forgiving others who have wronged us.

In addition to Matthew 5:7-9, this matrix of themes of mercy, compassion, and forgiveness occurs repeatedly. In Matthew 6 one of the spiritual practices to be done with a whole heart is giving alms or showing mercy to those in physical need (6:1-4), the opposite of which is the harsh judging that is condemned in 7:1-5. Jesus places great weight on showing compassion to others in need as highlighted twice with Matthew's strategic use of Hosea 6:6 (Matthew 9:13; 12:7)—"I desire mercy/compassion, not sacrifice." Closely related, Matthew regularly emphasizes that Jesus had compassion toward others in both emotion and action.

Five times in Matthew, Jesus is described as being full of compassion (directly in 9:36; 14:14; 15:32; 20:34; indirectly in 18:27). This is what motivates Him to heal people of all kinds of diseases and afflictions. By way of contrast, Jesus's conflict with His self-appointed enemies, the scribes and Pharisees, often centers on their lack of compassion for others (12:1-14; 23:4,23). Jesus regularly commands His disciples to show mercy (9:13; 12:7; 23:23; 18:21-35; 25:31-46) and He models it (9:27-31; 15:21-28; 17:14-18; 20:29-34). Also connected, Jesus repeatedly speaks of the necessity and beauty of forgiving other people who have sinned against us, often tying this to receiving forgiveness from God Himself (6:14-15; 18:15-20,35). Forgiveness toward those who have wronged us is central to being a disciple of Jesus because it is living in the way that God Himself does (5:45). Those who live in these ways of mercy, compassion, and forgiveness "will be called sons of God" (5:9).

The Beatitude in Matthew 5:8 is in many ways the most central, but it is also easily misunderstood. "Purity of heart" on the English ear sounds as if Jesus is referring to moral purity, especially evocative of sexual purity. While the Scriptures do speak of the importance of sexual purity in plenty of places, the meaning here is different. *Purity* here **means wholeness or consistency**—purity in the way that a silver ingot is more or less pure silver. To the degree to which it is mixed with other metals, it is not pure sliver. Jesus's point here taps into the main theme of the Sermon overall—righteousness as wholeness, as consistency between our internal and external lives. Specifically in the context of this triad of Beatitudes we understand Jesus exhorting us to lives of loyalty and integrity toward others, keeping purity in our relationships by not judging or condemning others (7:1-5). Because this is how God Himself is, with no shifting shadow in relation to us (James 1:17), Jesus promises that as we live in this kind of purity, we will see God Himself.

If we're not shocked yet by Jesus's topsy-turvy definitions of where to find true life, the last part of Jesus's Beatitudes will wake us up.

> *Blessed are those who are persecuted because of righteousness, for the kingdom of heaven is theirs. "You are blessed when they insult you and persecute you and falsely say every kind of evil against you because of me. Be glad and rejoice, because your reward is great in heaven. For that is how they persecuted the prophets who were before you.*
> MATTHEW 5:10-12

As we noted above, Matthew 5:10, which is the eighth macarism, is tied into the first one by repeating the phrase, "For the kingdom of heaven is theirs." This inclusio reminds us that **all of Jesus's teachings are an invitation into life in God's coming kingdom**. We can also observe that the central theme of the Sermon, righteousness, appears yet again. Just like the first set of four Beatitudes ends with longing for God's righteousness to come to the earth (5:6), now Jesus concludes the second set of four by speaking about what will happen when His disciples live in God's righteous ways—they will often experience unjust persecution, pain, and rejection. This is part of being kingdom citizens of heaven within a hostile earth.

This final message of the Beatitudes—that true happiness can be found even in the midst of unjust suffering—is doubly reinforced by Jesus's ninth and final macarism. This is the point of 5:11-12. Typical of many wisdom teachings in the ancient world, oftentimes a teacher would highlight the main point by expanding on the penultimate saying. That is, the eighth Beatitude wraps up the sequence with its repeated references to the kingdom and righteousness. Now the ninth Beatitude expands up this final one so that the most memorable takeaway is reiterated.

Jesus explains that His disciples will sooner or later experience the same things He did—insults, persecution, and false accusations. But contrary to our natural response, by faith we can learn to still experience flourishing and even joy. Why? Because **"your reward is great in heaven"** and we share in the communion of God's faithful prophets in the past (5:12).

Herein lies one of the most profound paradoxes of the Christian life—we can have genuine joy in the midst of suffering, rewards when it feels like loss, and life through death. Jesus models this in His own life and the New Testament authors return to this theme regularly (2 Corinthians 4:7-18; 1 Peter 1:3-12; James 1:2-18).

Life as Jesus's Priests in the World
MATTHEW 5:13-16

Jesus's teaching about salt and light is one of the many memorable sayings from the Sermon that has become influential, not only within the Church but in the broader world. But often such famous sayings are interpreted and applied without much knowledge of the context of the teaching. This is true of 5:13-16.

> *"You are the salt of the earth. But if the salt should lose its taste, how can it be made salty? It's no longer good for anything but to be thrown out and trampled under people's feet. "You are the light of the world. A city situated on a hill cannot be hidden. No one lights a lamp and puts it under a basket, but rather on a lampstand, and it gives light for all who are in the house. In the same way, let your light shine before others, so that they may see your good works and give glory to your Father in heaven.*
> **MATTHEW 5:13-16**

The first question is what these metaphors of "salt" and "light" mean. The short answer is that in the ancient world salt was used as analogy for a lot of different things. Light is also a widely used metaphor, especially in the Bible, but its meanings are more clearly defined. In the Bible, light often refers to God revealing Himself, which enables people to see. There is often a related moral sense, with light being connected to God and goodness in contrast with darkness.

If we pay attention to 5:13-15, we will see that Jesus puts these two metaphors in direct parallel with each other. These verses follow the same pattern. Jesus tells His disciples they are the "salt of the earth" which is paralleled with the "light of the world." This is followed by paired warnings to not let salt or light fail to meet their intended purposes. All of this shows we are supposed to interpret salt and light together, as mutually informing.

When we see the metaphors in parallel the meaning becomes clearer. **Salt and light are both images that connect to the role of priests in the Old Testament**—those who use salt in the making of covenants and who teach God's revelation. Jesus's point is that His disciples are now the priests and heralds of the new covenant God is making with the world through Jesus. As Jesus's disciples go into the world and shine the light of the gospel, through both word and deed, people will see God and (many) will glorify Him (5:16).

This is an incredible and weighty privilege. So why the warnings? Jesus ended His Beatitudes on a dark note—expect persecution, rejection, and suffering. In light of this unexpected and unpleasant prospect, Jesus must exhort His followers to remain faithful in the midst of hardship.

1.   Augustine, *The City of God*, trans. Marcus Dods, with introduction by Thomas Merton (New York: Modern Library, 1950).

Oil Lamp
ILLUSTRATOR PHOTO/ TOM HOOKE

Personal Reflection

Make a list of what you think would make you truly happy. How does this list compare to the things Jesus talks about in the Beatitudes?

From the first part of each Beatitude, consider the character traits that Jesus calls us to, such as humility, mercy, and peacemaking. Prayerfully examine your life and heart. Which of these do you see growing in your life? Which of these do you struggle with the most?

Persecution, fear, and suffering can tempt us to stop being salt and light in the world—to "lose our flavor" and to hide. Is there a situation in your life right now where fear is a more powerful factor than faithfulness in your witness?

2

THE GREATER RIGHTEOUSNESS OF THE KINGDOM

MATTHEW 5:17-48

In 2010 Susan Gregory published a best-selling book entitled *The Daniel Fast: Feed Your Soul, Strengthen Your Spirit, and Renew Your Body*. This book outlines a twenty-one-day diet plan (complete with recipes) that is based on the story of Daniel and his companions when they were taken captive by the Babylonian king Nebuchadnezzar.[1] Daniel 1:12-16 tells us that these men of God rejected the king's luxurious food and wine and instead only ate beans, fruits, vegetables, whole grains, and water. The result was they were healthier than ever. Many people in recent years have adopted this as their own diet. It appears to have some real health benefits. And for many Christians, it has the added benefit of being "biblical"—it's right there in the Bible.

If you start researching the "Daniel Fast" or "Biblical Diet" you will discover a whole world of websites, books, and blogs dedicated to teaching God's plan for food and how to eat biblically. These are based on various parts of the Old Testament—stories like Daniel's as well as the very detailed instructions in the Mosaic covenant about clean and unclean foods.

This raises an important question: Do these diet plans based on instructions given to Israel apply to Christians today? Apart from whatever potential health benefits there may be from avoiding shellfish and using lots of olive oil, are Christians required to follow these Old Testament food restrictions?

This question is really a version of a much bigger question: What teachings from the Old Testament apply to Christians today? The Hebrew Scriptures are full of instructions from God to His people and Jesus is clearly presented as the Jewish Messiah. It seems reasonable to argue that because God has not changed, these teachings from the Old Testament still apply to followers of Jesus. So are Christians forbidden to get tattoos

(Leviticus 19:28) and eat pork (Deuteronomy 14:8)? Are we required to circumcise boys on the eighth day (Genesis 17:9-14) and avoid working on the Sabbath/Saturday so that we can worship God (Exodus 20:8-11)?

These are hard questions. Christians have wrestled, debated, and disagreed on how to answer them from the very beginning. The New Testament itself records stories of Christian leaders struggling to figure out how to navigate these complex questions that often got very heated (Galatians 2:11-14; Acts 15:1-29).

Jesus's teachings in Matthew 5:17-20 don't answer every particular version of this question—we need to put the whole Bible together to do that—but what Jesus says here gives us the single most important contribution to this complicated issue.

The Sermon is a carefully crafted literary whole and 5:17-20 are not separate from the verses around them. Rather, 5:17-20 provides the thesis statement or guiding argument for the whole central section of the Sermon (5:17–7:12). In this portion of the study we will be looking at 5:17-48, which includes Jesus's big idea in 5:17-20 and the first set of six teachings to explain and apply this to our daily lives (5:21-48). Overall, in 5:17-48 Jesus is teaching us (1) how His entering into the world both confirms and transforms God's instructions to Israel; and (2) how to live righteously, that is, pleasing to God.

Not Abolish but Fulfill
MATTHEW 5:17-20

Jesus's famous Sermon began with a description of what true happiness in relationship to God looks like (5:1-16). Most of the things Jesus describes as states of true happiness are completely unexpected—humility, mourning, giving up one's rights for the sake of making peace—but are proven to be true when experienced in relationship with God. Jesus concluded by saying that His disciples would paradoxically find true life when they suffer for being righteous (5:10-12), which looks like good works as salt and light (5:13-16).

Building upon this introduction, Jesus now presses into the main topic of His message—**what it means to be righteous, that is, what it means to live according to what God says is right**. The connection is clear—God cares about our flourishing and this can only be found when we live according to God's ways.

Jesus's focus on righteousness is found in 5:20 and will be repeated through the Sermon. Even as the Beatitudes describe happiness in unexpected ways, what Jesus says about righteousness is shocking—"For I tell you, unless your righteousness surpasses that of the scribes and Pharisees, you will never get into the kingdom of heaven" (5:20).

It is not shocking that Jesus connects being righteous with entering the kingdom of heaven. That is consistent teaching throughout the Bible. The unexpected and even dismaying aspect of Jesus's statement is that kingdom-entering people must have a greater righteousness than the scribes and Pharisees. Why is this problematic? Because the scribes and Pharisees in Jesus's day were the theological and moral conservatives, the holy people. They were the educated, pious leaders among God's people. They were known for their intensive study of God's laws and their obedience to every detail. From a Jewish perspective they were the most righteous people. And yet we are told we must have a greater righteousness than theirs. This would be like saying to a local congregation today, "If you want to be part of God's kingdom, you need to be way more holy and theologically educated than our best missionaries and pastors."

What is Jesus saying? The rest of His teachings in 5:21–7:12 will unpack what He means by this startling claim. We'll come back to this momentarily. But before He explains what He means through a series of examples, He needs to clarify something crucial about who He is and what His coming into the world means.

This clarification is found in 5:17-19:

> *Don't think that I came to abolish the Law or the Prophets.*
> *I did not come to abolish but to fulfill. For truly I tell*
> *you, until heaven and earth pass away, not the smallest*
> *letter or one stroke of a letter will pass away from the*
> *law until all things are accomplished. Therefore, whoever*
> *breaks one of the least of these commands and teaches*
> *others to do the same will be called least in the kingdom*
> *of heaven. But whoever does and teaches these commands*
> *will be called great in the kingdom of heaven.*
> MATTHEW 5:17-19

There are several important truths we learn from Jesus's words here:

First, **Jesus the Messiah has not come into the world to disregard, critique, overturn, or destroy God's previous revelation**. He is not unhitching the New Testament from the Old Testament as if He is embarrassed by it. He is not abolishing God's former revelation that was given beginning with the book of Genesis. The Old Testament remains crucial to the Christian two-testament Bible and theology. This is His point in 5:17—**"I did not come to abolish."**

This is also what He is saying in the potentially confusing words of 5:18-19. Using several poetic images (**"Heaven and earth passing away,"** **"The smallest stroke of a letter,"** **"Least and greatest in the kingdom of heaven"**) Jesus affirms the abiding witness of all that God has spoken in the past to Abraham, Moses, David, and the prophets. Anyone who interprets Jesus as abolishing or neglecting God's words misunderstands Him and is not a kingdom disciple. He will say the same thing in His final sparring with the Pharisees in Matthew 23—**"you have neglected the more important matters of the law—justice, mercy, and faithfulness. These things should have been done without neglecting the others"** (23:23). There is no rejection of God's revelation to the Jewish people.

However, He doesn't stop there. He did not come to abolish God's instructions, but He is also not merely a prophet repeating what God has said before. We must keep reading 5:17—"I did not come to abolish but to fulfill." In addition to affirming that He is not abolishing God's instructions about being righteous (shorthand—"the Law or the Prophets"), He explains that something is changing. Things aren't going to just stay the same with His entry into the world. He has come to "fulfill" the Law and the Prophets. (See the Closer Look on "Fulfillment.")

Now we can return to Jesus's shocking statement in 5:20, that our righteousness needs to surpass that of the scribes and Pharisees. As we noted above, this is a disturbing prospect because (1) the scribes and Pharisees were by all accounts godly and pious people, (2) when we take an honest look at our lives we know we fail in many ways, and (3) this sounds like God is putting an impossible burden on us.

When we keep reading to the end of this section of Jesus's teachings, we don't get any more assurance. Jesus concludes with another strong statement—"Be perfect, therefore, as your heavenly Father is perfect" (5:48).

A CLOSER LOOK

Fulfillment

Scholars of the Gospel of Matthew have observed that the single word that best sums up Matthew's theology is *fulfillment*. This weighty word ties together much of what Matthew is communicating.

But this accurate observation needs more explanation. What does it mean for Jesus to bring about the fulfillment of God's work in the world? What does Matthew mean by this word? We can't just assume that our use of the English word matches his point. We need to look closely at how he clarifies this crucial biblical idea.

In Matthew's introductory chapters he relates several stories about Jesus's entry into the world (Matthew 1–2). For each story he explains that this event "fulfills" some aspect of the Old Testament. This reiterates the idea that Jesus's story is not disconnected from the story of Israel. At the same time Matthew pulls Israel's story forward to its intended goal that has now come to fruition in Jesus.

When we look at how Jesus's story fulfills the Old Testament in Matthew 1–2 we see that fulfillment is a rich and multi-layered idea. On the one hand, Jesus coming into the world was predicted by God's prophets of old (1:22-23; 2:5-6). At the same time, Jesus's story should also be understood not just as a prediction but also by way of analogy—the things that happened to Jesus as an infant are reminiscent of things that had happened to God's people before. They weren't predicted but they do resonate and rhyme (2:15,17-18,23). These resonances can only be seen retrospectively, after we reflect on Jesus's life after the resurrection.

Understanding this multi-layered meaning of *fulfill* helps us understand how the New Testament rereads the whole Old Testament in light of Jesus (see also Luke 24:44-45). All that God has said and done now finds its truest and fullest meaning through Jesus Christ.

This is the context to understand that Jesus has not come to abolish the law but "fulfill" it. He is affirming the authority of God's speech in the past while also explaining that a new and final era is arriving through Him.

This one-two punch of high demands has led many readers, like Martin Luther, to interpret Jesus's teachings not as real expectations for us to respond to but rather as statements that show us our utter inability to please God. For Luther and many after him, these declarations are meant to make us flee from any self-reliance and seek Christ's imputed righteousness.

While Luther is right that we cannot earn salvation with God through doing righteous things and that we need Christ's imputed righteousness, this is not what Jesus is talking about in 5:20-48. Jesus uses the word *righteousness* in its more common biblical sense of "doing what is right" or "doing God's will." Jesus is not talking here about the idea of imputed legal standing.

Rather, a righteousness that "surpasses that of the scribes and Pharisees" means something deeper—**God wants our lives to be marked by a consistency between our external lives and our internal persons, a wholeness between our actions and our hearts.** This is what the summary word in 5:48 means. To be "perfect" (Greek, *teleios*) does not in Greek mean "free from fault" but whole and consistent. Jesus's call to have a greater righteousness than the scribes and Pharisees is an invitation to wholeness and integrity, even as God the Father Himself is.

With this understanding we can now read the set of six examples in 5:21-48. These six examples of **"greater righteousness"** have a consistent theme—Jesus is calling us to wholeness, to a life where our external behavior matches our interior hearts. Jesus is showing that to fulfill all righteousness is to follow God's commands not just externally (which is good) but also with a heart connected to Him (contrast this with Isaiah 29:13 quoted in Matthew 15:8-9).

Many interpreters have called this section Jesus's "Antitheses" because at first glance Jesus seems to be contrasting what He is saying with the commands of the Mosaic law—"You've heard it said but I say to you"—repeated six times. But when we read them carefully and in light of 5:20 and 5:48 we will see that they are not antitheses to the Law but true explanations (exegesis) about what God said, coming to us from the Master Teacher who is a faithful prophet and more—the Son of God Himself, the final authority.

Murder and Anger
MATTHEW 5:21-26

In this first example Jesus reminds us of one of the Ten Commandments (Exodus 20:13; Deuteronomy 5:17)—do not murder. Nothing new here. We would all agree that the external action of murder is bad. But Jesus doesn't stop there:

"But I tell you, everyone who is angry with his brother or sister will be subject to judgment. Whoever insults his brother or sister will be subject to the court. Whoever says, 'You fool!' will be subject to hellfire" (Matthew 5:22).

What does this mean? Jesus's point is not that murder and hatred are equally bad. They're not! The physical, relational, legal, and moral consequences of murder will always be greater than hatred and resentment.

But Jesus is showing us that **we must not be content with merely external obedience.** We must pay attention to our inner person, what God sees and cares about. If our lives are marked by hatred and resentment, even though we may not physically murder someone, we show that we aren't really following God's way of love. Our hearts matter and reveal who we really are.

Adultery and Lust
MATTHEW 5:27-30

These verses give Jesus's second example of what "greater righteousness" looks like (5:20). Once again we see the issue is wholeness, not merely external obedience. The power of sexual sin is universal in human nature and society. Adultery is damaging to all involved, but **Jesus pushes His disciples to pursue something even beyond the avoidance of adultery— avoiding a lifestyle of lust.** He calls people to heart-level virtue.

Jesus helps us see that God has always seen and cared about our inner person, not merely our external behavior. God's people should have known this from the Ten Commandments alone. In Exodus 20:14, God says not to commit adultery, but He doesn't stop there. The tenth commandment drives the heart-focus point home:

"Do not covet your neighbor's house. Do not covet your neighbor's wife, his male or female servant, his ox or donkey, or anything that belongs to your neighbor" (Exodus 20:17).

Jesus uses violent images of tearing out eyes and cutting off hands (Matthew 5:29-30) not so that we will take these literally when we sin (though some Christians have unfortunately done so!) but so that we will wake up and feel the seriousness of these heart matters. As our teacher of true wisdom, Jesus warns against foolishness—**no temporary pleasure is worth missing the true life found in God's kingdom.**

Cut It Out

Which of the following would you cut out of your life for purity and integrity's sake? Put a (**Y**) before any activity you have chosen to forego at some point and a (**N**) in front of the non-negotiables to date. Match the activity you cut out with the sin or temptation it may have created.

___ Social media

___ Political discussions

___Films with graphic sex scenes

___Credit cards

___Alcohol consumption

___ Overspending

___ Drunkenness/
alcoholism

___ Lust

___ Envy

___ Anger or judgment

What else would you add to this list?

Adultery and Divorce
MATTHEW 5:31-32

With the first two examples Jesus has established the pattern of His point—**we need both external and internal godliness.** In this third example of greater righteousness, He enters into the debate regarding possible justifications for divorce. The rabbinic schools of Jesus's day had diverging opinions about how loose or strict the allowances for divorce should be. Many rabbis said that one could be righteous in divorcing one's spouse for almost any reason that caused offense. Others were more strict. Jesus more closely aligns with the latter group. Later in Matthew, Jesus will be more specific about the allowable situations, noting that marriage is meant to be lifelong (Matthew 19:1-12).

This third example of greater righteousness is closely related to the second one (5:27-30). While the action of divorce and remarriage are clearly external behaviors (as with murder and adultery), the point is the same: the real issue is the heart of the one causing the divorce. When Jesus returns to the issue of divorce, remarriage, and adultery, this is what He explicitly says—**"Moses permitted you to divorce your wives because of the hardness of your hearts, but it was not like that from the beginning"** (19:8). Once again, our tendency is to focus on the external behavior, but Jesus is challenging us to look inside at the heart matter.

Oaths and Words
MATTHEW 5:33-37

Words are powerful. It is through speaking that God created the world. As creatures made in His image, our speech matters too. Often in the name of religion people make righteous-sounding commitments, but we also often fail to do them or make these oaths with impure motives.

In this fourth example of what the "greater righteousness" looks like, Jesus once again emphasizes the necessity of connecting our outward actions with our inner person, our outward speech and our heart-level commitments. Particularly Jesus points out the tendency of the scribes and Pharisees (and us too) to focus on minute details and hair-splitting distinctions that can be made to enable one to navigate around wholehearted commitment to do what we say we're going to do. This is so important that Jesus will return to this issue in 23:16-22. In that expanded version of 5:33-37, He will again point out ways in which we skirt around our commitments. While making fine distinctions about an oath made by "the temple" versus "the gold of the temple" (23:16-17) may serve some technical purpose, they reveal a heart problem.

Any attempt to manipulate words to make subtle, self-serving distinctions are less than the required whole-person righteousness. What we say must be what we believe and do. This is the virtue of wholeness in speech.

The letter of James picks up on this theme from Jesus and uses it throughout. James 1:19-20 succinctly states, **"My dear brothers and sisters, understand this: Everyone should be quick to listen, slow to speak, and slow to anger, for human anger does not accomplish God's righteousness."** James 3:1-12 reminds us of the power of the tongue and the need to control it and use it for good. And James 5:12 reiterates Jesus's command most clearly—**"Above all, my brothers and sisters, do not swear, either by heaven or by earth or with any other oath. But let your 'yes' mean 'yes,' and your 'no' mean 'no,' so that you won't fall under judgment."** A good application of Matthew 5:33-37 would be to say less and promise less, always considering in your heart before speaking with your mouth.

Retaliation and Vengeance
MATTHEW 5:38-42

Inherent in the human heart is the impulse to retaliation, to return hurt for hurt, pain for pain, evil for evil. From the first act of violence in the Bible (Cain and Abel in Genesis 4) till today, this is the way of sinful humanity. As we saw with the commandment prohibiting murder (which is also alluding to the Cain and Abel story), the deeper issue is our hearts—our propensity toward anger, resentment, and hatred (5:21-26). Jesus addresses this heart issue with His fifth example of the greater righteousness that is necessary to enter His kingdom. The call to not retaliate and indeed, to outdo evil with good, is related to several of Jesus's Beatitudes, including the call to be merciful (5:7) and a peacemaker (5:9).

Going beyond the call to not take our own vengeance (5:38-39), Jesus gives an example of how to live in the opposite way—giving generously to those who demand or ask things of us (5:40-42). As with all of Jesus's examples, we need wisdom to know how and when to practice such principles. But the moral vision is clear—**we can and should practice ways of relating to our enemies that reflect an inward heart of love.**

Enemies and Love
MATTHEW 5:43-48

Sadly, tension and conflict between people is the universal human experience. This theme appears repeatedly throughout all six examples. Anger and resentment between "brothers and sisters" is the focus of 5:21-26. Not retaliating against those demanding or asking something of us is addressed in 5:38-42. And now, in the final escalation of these commands, we are told to love our enemies. This is the sixth and climactic example of what whole-person righteousness looks like according to Jesus.

According to Jesus, love for God is the greatest commandment and the organically-related love for others is the second (Matthew 22:34-40). The basis for this way of being in the world is likeness to God Himself. Humans are made in the image of God and therefore we function most fully in our humanity when we imitate and reflect God. This is called an ethic of imitation or virtue. The Father God blesses and cares for the righteous and the unrighteous (5:45). Therefore, His children should do so as well.

As cracked and marred images of God we now find it natural to do the opposite—to give ourselves over to hatred, resentment, retribution, and vengeance. Jesus calls His disciples to recognize and reconnect to our nature as children of God. Rather than hatred, we are called to love, to treat even our enemies as we would want to be treated (see also 7:12). Anyone can be friendly to those who are friendly to them (5:46-47). God's call is higher and deeper—to love even our enemies.

All of 5:21-48 is summed up in the concluding verse—**"Be perfect, therefore, as your heavenly Father is perfect"** (5:48). Unfortunately, the translation "perfect" is problematic. In English this makes it sound like God expects us to live sinless lives. Not only is this impossible while living as fallen creatures in a fallen world, this view is based on a misunderstanding of what Jesus is saying here. This misunderstanding has led to grievous burdens being put upon Christians, ironically like the Pharisees did in Jesus's day (23:4). It has also led to a misreading of the whole Sermon on the Mount, interpreting it as if it has nothing positive to instruct us, but only shows us our sinfulness. Neither of these readings understand correctly what Jesus is saying.

The word translated into English here as "perfect" is meant to communicate the idea of maturity, completion, and wholeness. There is a family of Greek words that all come from this same root and **they speak to the goodness of when humans operate with integrity and**

consistency, with learned wisdom that comes from maturity (see James 1:4,17; Hebrews 2:10; 5:9; 1 Corinthians 2:6; Ephesians 4:13; and many others). The idea is not that disciples will be perfect in their behavior or hearts but that we must be "whole" or "completely dedicated." There is a difference between wholeness and flawlessness. To focus on being flawless would be to fall back into the external-focused error of the Pharisees. **The goal of wholeness directs our energy toward integrating our external and internal lives.** Our wholeness and goodness will never be fully consistent like God's because of our limits and our sinfulness. But we are still called to grow in imitating our Father.

The sixth and final example of greater righteousness is the highest and most comprehensive one: the call to love. This addresses the same topic of the first example (Matthew 5:21-26) but here is stated positively. This greater righteousness is rooted in God's own nature. God loves even His enemies and so His children must do the same.

View of the Sea of Galilee from the Mount of Beatitudes, Sea of Galilee, Israel
ILLUSTRATOR PHOTO/G.B. HOWELL

Truth or Dare

The series of statements that Jesus proclaimed in the Sermon on the Mount upended His audience's expectations, either because of the astonishing perfectionism they seemed to contain or their paradoxical truths.

What's your gut response to these claims?

Put an X on the line to show whether you accept Jesus's words as unvarnished Truth or something that seems much closer to a Dare, a statement that seriously challenges your ability to conform to it.

TRUTH · DARE

Our lives should not be marked by
bitterness and resentment.

TRUTH · DARE

Lust is equal to adultery.

TRUTH · DARE

We are to relate to our enemies
with compassion and love.

TRUTH · DARE

Christians are to be perfect (whole and consistent).

Are there any that challenge your faith to the point of rejection? What can you do to come to the same understanding as Jesus and take His teachings to heart?

Summing It Up
MATTHEW 5:17-20

This first part of the main body of the Sermon is thick with big ideas and challenging words. It will be helpful to recall that the heart of the Sermon is found in 5:17–7:12, with 5:17-20 serving as the governing words over it all. In 5:17-20 Jesus clarifies that He is not abolishing what God said in the past but, quite the opposite, **He is explaining what God's intent in the Law always was and that He is bringing all of God's work and words to completion in Himself,** the One incarnate Son of God. He describes all of this with the weighty word *fulfillment*.

What was God's intent in the Law? That we be righteous. This does not mean that we be legalistic but that we humbly, sincerely, and prayerfully seek to be whole people, paying attention both to our external behaviors and especially our internal postures. This is the "greater righteousness" that is necessary for us to be a part of God's coming kingdom (5:20).

In Matthew 5:21-48 Jesus helps us see how God's call for us to be whole is worked out in regard to several of the commands we find in the Old Testament. Jesus's teachings in the remainder of the main part of the Sermon (6:1–7:12) will continue this same theme, applying the wholeness theme to other aspects of our lives.

Personal Reflection

Jesus's words about anger, lust, keeping our word, and loving our enemies hit hard. It is not difficult to feel the pinch of Jesus's challenge. But we shouldn't collapse under a sense of guilt and shame. Jesus invites us to live as God has made us and thereby find life. With this vision, we may press into some heart-level questions:

Reflect on a recent time when you were angry, hateful, and/or spoke against someone else. What motivated this? Be honest before the Lord.

What can you do to reconcile with this person?

Divorces never happen in one day, but come from seeds of destruction that are planted and grow choking weeds. If you are married, examine your heart and renew your commitment to live in faithfulness and forgiveness toward your spouse. Resist the subtle ways in which we give ourselves over to lust such as imagining being with someone other than our God-given spouse.

If you are married, what is one step you can take to secure your marriage?

Do you have any enemies? Maybe not in the normal sense of that word, but can you think of someone you struggle to forgive or you know doesn't like you. Loving those who have hurt us is extremely difficult to do in our own power. Pray for God's Spiritual power to grant you a forgiving heart, and then step toward forgiving those who have wronged you.

Write a prayer below.

1.   Susan Gregory, *The Daniel Fast: Feed Your Soul, Strengthen Your Spirit, and Renew Your Body* (Carol Stream, IL: Tyndale House, 2009).

3

OUR PRAISE PROBLEM

MATTHEW 6:1-21

We humans have a praise problem. Our praise problem works in two directions, the vertical and the horizontal. Our vertical praise problem is that we often love and worship created things rather than the Creator (Romans 1:21-23). This dishonors our God and distorts our souls. The great theologian Augustine helpfully describes sin as our "disordered loves"[1]—we love and worship in a disordered way, loving the wrong things or loving good things but in the wrong degree and order.

But we also have a horizontal praise problem—we all long for the praise and recognition of others. The issue here is complicated. On the one hand, there is nothing wrong with this in that we are designed as communal creatures who need each other's love, affirmation, and encouragement. Any human who never receives this kind of good "praise" will not thrive physically, emotionally, or relationally. Additionally, God has made the world in such a way that we cannot help but praise and honor good and beautiful things in our fellow humans—a beautifully played violin sonata, a perfect goal in the corner of the net in a soccer game, an act of heroism or kindness. These things and these people rightly deserve honor, praise, and accolades.

But on the other hand, just like all our other loves, this good need for praise can get distorted. Our desire for the praise that comes from others can become disordered and we can become dependent on and crave this kind of attention, like an addict.

Here in Matthew 6:1-21, Jesus addresses this disordered desire for the praise that comes from other people, applying it particularly to our religious lives. As with the rest of the Sermon, the point is the same—God wants us to be whole people, people whose outward lives match our inward lives, even as God Himself is whole and consistent (5:48).

Reorienting Us to the Sermon's Main Idea

We are continuing in the main body of Jesus's famous Sermon on the Mount (5:17–7:12). The theme that ties this section together is there is a "greater righteousness" in relationship to God and others that is required to enter into the kingdom of heaven (5:20). This greater righteousness is not us trying to perform more to earn favor with God or do more super spiritual activities. **The greater righteousness Jesus is talking about is wholeness, completeness, integrity, and harmony between our outer behavior and our inner person, or our heart.**

Jesus is always welcoming and always practical. He doesn't just deal in the abstract. In 5:21-48 He gives six examples of what this greater righteousness/wholeness looks like—paying attention to lust, anger, greed, and so forth in our inner person, not just focusing on the external behavior (which also matters!) but on the root of our outer behavior, which is who we are on the inside.

Here in chapter 6, Jesus continues to invite us to think about our lives in light of our inner person. This time He applies this truth to our spiritual practices, our religious piety, via three examples. In each of these three examples—giving to help the poor, prayer, and fasting—Jesus teaches the same thing again: don't just focus on the outward behavior, but pay attention to your heart, your motives, and beware that our hearts are often motivated by the praise of others in an unhealthy way.

The Opening Exhortation
MATTHEW 6:1

Good teaching often goes from a general principle to specific applications. There are several places in Matthew where Jesus teaches this way, including here in 6:1-21. The general heading is stated in 6:1. This will be matched with a concluding exhortation in 6:19-21. In 6:2-18 Jesus gives us three particular applications of the principle.

So what is the principle exhortation?

"Be careful not to practice your righteousness in front of others to be seen by them. Otherwise, you have no reward with your Father in heaven" (6:1).

The basic idea is clear—if we do righteous things with the motive of being seen and praised by others, God will not reward us. Jesus will explain more what this means through His three examples.

This heading verse says a couple of things we're not used to hearing. First, note that there is no doubt that we should be doing or practicing righteousness. Jesus expects us to be engaged in certain activities that can be described as **"practicing righteousness."** The question is how and why we do these things. This connects us back to 5:20 and Jesus's statement that we need to be righteous in a way that is greater than the scribes and Pharisees. (See Closer Look on "Righteousness" below.)

The second surprising idea from 6:1 is this talk of having a reward with our Father in heaven. Jesus often speaks about God rewarding people for their faithfulness. This is an especially frequent theme in Matthew, where the language of reward/recompense (5:12,46; 6:1-2,5,16; 10:41-42; 16:27; 20:8) and treasure (6:19-21; 12:35; 13:44,52; 19:21) occur regularly. Disciples do not earn favor with God by merely doing righteous things, but God does honor and bless His people for their faithful and obedient response to Jesus. (See also the parable of the talents in Matthew 25:14-30.) Despite how frequent of an idea this is, we don't often think of God rewarding us for our faithfulness, or we diminish this idea by thinking of it in vague spiritual terms. While we don't know exactly what that "reward" will look like in the new creation, we cannot deny the mechanism that God has established—that what we do does affect our future compensation from God. This same reward theme is how 6:1-21 ends, with Jesus inviting us to live wisely by storing up treasures/rewards with God in heaven, not with humans on earth.

Jewish Scribe on Mt. Zion near David's Tomb
ILLUSTRATOR PHOTO/LOUISE KOHL SMITH

A CLOSER LOOK

Righteousness

We've already noted that the main idea that drives the central section of the Sermon is that we need to have a righteousness that is greater than the scribes and Pharisees. Apart from this we cannot enter into the kingdom of heaven (5:20).

Righteousness is a frequent and important theme in Matthew. The Greek root for "righteous" (*dikai-*) appears twenty-six times in Matthew. It is often used to refer to "the righteous ones," an important category of people, the disciples. Six of the occurrences of the "righteous" root appear in the Sermon (5:6,10,20,45; 6:1,33), including in two of the Beatitudes: those hungering and thirsting for righteousness (5:6) and those persecuted because of righteousness (5:10).

Since the time of the Reformation, many have assumed that the Protestant understanding of righteousness in Paul's letters—righteousness as a legal standing—is also what Matthew means. Thus, for example, "hungering and thirsting for righteousness" is often interpreted as longing for the salvation God gives.

But careful study has shown that the Old Testament roots of the idea of righteousness are larger and more nuanced. In the Old Testament "righteous" often has the idea of restorative justice, that is, God's work of setting the world to right. This is His saving activity that we participate in and benefit from.

The most common and basic sense of "righteous" or "righteousness" in both the Old and New Testaments refers simply to doing what is right, living in the ways that God has revealed. The normal sense of righteousness means doing God's will. We can never earn our way into God's covenant by doing good things, but God's people are still called to and expected to do His will, to do what is right, to practice righteousness.

This common biblical meaning of "righteousness" is how Jesus uses the idea in Matthew. We can define righteousness in Matthew as **"whole-person behavior that accords with God's nature, will, and coming kingdom."** The righteous person, according to Matthew, is the one who follows Jesus in this way of being in the world. The righteous person is the whole/*teleios* person (5:48) who does not only do the will of God externally but, most importantly, from the heart.

Once we understand this principle it will make sense of the frequent invitation from Jesus to become His disciples, to be "trained in righteousness," as Paul will later describe it in 2 Timothy 3:16.

The First Example: Almsgiving
MATTHEW 6:2-4

Jesus is inviting us to reorient our thinking to correspond with what God cares about—our hearts that flow out into a good life, not merely external obedience. Sadly and ironically, even in the realm of religious practices we can miss God's call, focusing on external activities rather than the motives and heart underneath.

Jesus gives three examples (of the many He could give) of good spiritual practices that have the potential to be lived out with wrong motives. The first of these is the practice of almsgiving. Almsgiving is not the same thing as tithes and other sacrifices God's people make to support the ministry of the church. Rather, almsgiving is specifically giving money and doing services that help the poor and needy, whether they be the sick, the elderly, orphans, or widows. Almsgiving is an intentional acting out of mercy and compassion for those in need, something God models and commends.

In 6:3 Jesus says that our giving to those in need should be done in secret, and that we should not **"let [our] left hand know what [our] right hand is doing."** He does not mean that all our serving must be anonymous, as if we would need to wear a ski mask when helping someone move or only give cash gifts so one at church knows how much your offering was. After all, Jesus has already said that our good works should shine out so that people will give glory to God (see 5:16). Rather than requiring anonymous almsgiving, Jesus is challenging our motives for doing this righteous deed. If we are doing these things to get praise from others rather than out of love, then we lack the wholeness and true righteousness He wants for us. But when we do seek to do good to bless others rather than manipulate them into giving us praise, God will Himself reward us (6:4).

The Second Example: Prayer
MATTHEW 6:5-8

Continuing with the same idea, Jesus then talks about praying, once again challenging us to pay attention to our hearts and not just our lips. Whole-person, greater-righteousness praying will not be in the way that the Pharisees pray. Their kind of praying has two problems. First, it is focused on public appearance—**"Standing in the synagogues and on the street corners to be seen by people"** (6:5). Second, their kind of praying (which Jesus ironically calls being like the Gentiles), piles up lots of fancy-sounding prayer words (6:7). It is a "babbling" that assumes that their outward performance of prayer will be effective. **It fails to understand that prayer is approaching God as a Father who knows our needs and cares** (6:9). He's not interested in being manipulated by incantations.

Jesus calls those who practice this outward-focused praying "hypocrites" (6:5). In Matthew, Jesus frequently criticizes scribes and Pharisees as hypocrites (6:2,5,16; 7:5; 15:7; 22:18; 23:13,15,23,25,27,29; 24:51). We typically use the word *hypocrite* to mean someone who doesn't practice what they preach. Jesus's use of the word is more subtle, powerful, and convicting. **The hypocrites in Matthew are those who are actually doing good and righteous deeds but who lack wholeness and a heart dedicated to God.** They have the external righteousness without the internal, and therefore no true righteousness. We can be this kind of hypocrite even with eloquent prayers.

The Lord's Prayer
MATTHEW 6:9-15

The Sermon on the Mount contains many "greatest hits"—sayings and images from Jesus that are widely known. But none compares with Matthew 6:9-15, the Lord's Prayer (or "Our Father" in many traditions and other languages). Luke also has a shorter version of this same prayer (Luke 11:2-4) but it was Matthew's that quickly became the standard and made its way into the church's liturgy and practice. Most people of Christian faith throughout the world today pray these specific words at least every Sunday and many every day.

This is not an accident or mere coincidence. From a literary perspective, the Lord's Prayer is central to the whole Sermon. Matthew's literary skill and intentionality is seen once again in the way he highlights the prayer. The Sermon consists of three parts—an introduction (5:1-16), main body (5:17–7:12), and conclusion (7:13–8:1). Within the main body there are three sections (5:17-48; 6:1-21; 6:19–7:12), and within the middle of these sections (6:1-21), we find three examples. In the middle of these is the Lord's Prayer, putting Jesus's words here in the middle of the middle of the middle of the Sermon!

This literary centrality matches its theological and practical import. In the Lord's Prayer, Jesus teaches His disciples the fundamental way to think about their relationship to the heavenly Father as well as their daily lives. The prayer functions not only as a guide for our praying but also to reshape our sensibilities and perspective.

The Lord's Prayer is broken into two parts, much like the Ten Commandments. These two parts **look in two different directions: the first looks vertically, up to God; the second looks horizontally, toward our daily lives and relationships with others.**

The first, vertical set of petitions concerns God's name, fame, and glory being upheld (6:9-10). Jesus directs His disciples to look to God as Father, even as He does. Our initial petitions are for the Father to make what is true in heaven become the full reality on earth. There is a tension between the heavenly realm and the earthly, between God's perfect heavenly reign and the brokenness and sinfulness of the world around us. The Christian is one who is looking up and forward to the time and place when God's name will be honored, His kingdom realized, and His will done fully, "On earth as it is in heaven."

The second, horizontal set of petitions relates to the daily life of the believer: God's provision of daily needs, receiving God's forgiveness and extending it to others, and being spared from trials that will test us to the point of tempting God (6:11-13). The necessity of loving relationships is emphasized by its repetition at the end of the prayer with the requirement of forgiveness toward others (6:14-15).

The Christian life is very much oriented around the Lord's Prayer—it teaches us that we are living as sojourners and strangers in this world, looking for and longing for God's kingdom to come from heaven to earth and to set the world (and us) to right. This posture should mark all of our prayers and our living as disciples of Jesus—we are living on earth awaiting God to return from heaven and reestablish His good and beautiful kingdom. As we sojourn and wait, we live in daily dependence on God and in loving relationships with others.

The Lord's Prayer is not a magical incantation nor the only set of petitions that Christians pray. Some have described it as a scaffolding as we build a tower of prayer, or handrails as we ascend the stairs of prayer. In these ways the prayer can and should become an organic part of our lives of following Jesus.

The Lost Art of Fasting

Faith people depicted in the Bible practiced fasting with intentionality. Read the passages below to identify who and why.

	Person	Purpose
Exodus 34:28		
Esther 4:15-16		
Jonah 3:5-9		
Daniel 10:1-3		
2 Samuel 1:11-12		
Luke 4:1-3		
Acts 13:1-3		

The Third Example: Fasting
MATTHEW 6:16-18

In his third and final example of what wholeness/true holiness looks like in our practices of piety, Jesus addresses the practice of fasting. **Fasting is the practice of abstaining from food to dedicate oneself to prayer, meditation, and study.** Sometimes people fast for a specific need, such as deliverance from one's enemies or disease, for repentance, or for grief

(1 Samuel 1:7-8; 2 Samuel 1:12; 2 Chronicles 20:3; Esther 4:16; Matthew 4:2). Even though many Christians in the modern West do not fast, for many Christians, fasting is a regular habit, even as it was for the Pharisees in Jesus's day who fasted two days each week. Jesus expects His disciples to fast—"When you fast" not "If you happened to get around to fasting"— but focuses on the heart motive for doing so. If one fasts to get praise and honor from others then this does not please God or result in good for the one fasting.

As we have seen with the examples of almsgiving and prayer, we can and often do distort even the best of spiritual practices. The human heart is such that even in act of self-denial like fasting there is the possible corruption of motives, to performing this act for the purpose of receiving praise from others. Instead, Christians should be motivated by receiving God's rewards for their faithful dedication.

The Concluding Exhortation
MATTHEW 6:19-21

Jesus is a master teacher and by giving three examples with repeated phrases over and over, His point is inescapably clear—**God sees and cares about our motives.** He wants us to "practice our righteousness" in terms of these spiritual disciplines, but He also wants us to remember that mere outward performance neither honors our Father nor benefits our souls. God wants us to flourish, to partake in the "rewards" that come from living according to God's design for our lives.

All of this is reiterated and driven home in Jesus's concluding words to this section, 6:19-21. Jesus slightly changes the vocabulary from "reward" to "treasure" but the point is the same—we must not be so foolish as to live our lives for merely earthly treasures rather than heavenly ones. Hear again Jesus's words:

> *"Don't store up for yourselves treasures on earth, where moth and rust destroy and where thieves break in and steal. But store up for yourselves treasures in heaven, where neither moth nor rust destroys, and where thieves don't break in and steal. For where your treasure is, there your heart will be also."*
> **MATTHEW 6:19-21**

Notice that Jesus is not afraid to appeal to our greatest desire—for favor, blessing, and reward with God. There is nothing wrong with our desire for good and flourishing. God regularly exhorts us on this basis. Our problem is not our longing for "treasures in heaven" or "reward with our Father in heaven." Our problem is that we so often pursue the wrong goods— rewards and treasures that are temporary, corruptible, perishing, earthly.

This matters because what we give our hearts shapes who we become. This is what Jesus means in 6:21—"For where your treasure is, there your heart will be also." What we treasure—earthly versus heavenly things—will determine our destiny.

As we have noted, these three examples of "practicing righteousness" are just that, examples. Jesus is not giving us a comprehensive list of acts of spiritual piety. He is using these three examples to reshape our sensibilities and practices such that we resist the temptation to focus only on the outward acts and neglect what God really cares about, our hearts.

Upending Praise

What's a gracious way to make sure that God gets the glory?

Match the common praises we hear with a response that will help turn attention to God.

Thank you for your service.	Jesus is the perfect example. I follow Him.
You are so talented.	It is my joy and honor to serve Christ.
Your testimony is so moving.	The power is in God's living, breathing Word.
You know how to bring God's Word alive.	God did the work in my life.
You are such a good example of a Christian.	I can do nothing without Christ.

Personal Reflection

The Lord's Prayer is not a magical incantation, but it is good to pray this set prayer regularly, both privately and corporately, to help shape our sensibilities and habits in prayer. Maybe you haven't prayed the actual words of the Lord's Prayer very often because you are afraid of it being a mere ritual. While this is always a potential danger, the alternative is worse! Praying the Lord's Prayer meditatively and humbly before our Father is a good habit.

A good practice is to pray a line of the Lord's Prayer and then from that to pray other related prayers. You can start this today! Spend some time doing that now.

Jesus's teachings here are include an invitation to spend some dedicated time fasting from something in your life that has the potential to control you (food, media, and so forth). This is not a practice to earn favor with God, but it is an opportunity to grow in awareness of our ways in which we have become overly tied to "earthly treasures."

What is something you might fast from for a season?

Jesus's challenging words here are not meant to discourage us. If we're honest, when we look in our hearts we will always see mixed motives. We are never fully free from impurity even in our most pious acts. And even when we are close to purity in the act, it is easy to soon fall into pride and self-congratulations for being so pious! This does not mean we should be paralyzed and stop doing good things until we are perfect. This will never happen. Instead, when we look inside and see our impure and mixed motives, use this as an opportunity to turn again to the Lord in honest repentance, knowing that He has not come into the world to condemn us but to show us the way to find true and full life (John 3:17; 10:10).

Where might you have impure or mixed motives that you need to hand to Jesus and repent?

1.   Augustine, *The City of God*, trans. Marcus Dods, with introduction by Thomas Merton (New York: Modern Library, 1950).

4

THE BRIDGE TO WHOLENESS

MATTHEW 6:19-34

Growing up in the Midwest in the 1970s in a thoroughly middle-class family, we didn't eat much fresh fish. The only exceptions were pond-caught catfish from the occasional Cub Scout outing and, far preferable, the grease-laden adventure that was Long John Silver's. The kids' meals there were, appropriately, pirate themed, complete with a cardboard hat (of the tricorn variety) and the colorful cardboard treasure chest containing the fish, fries, and "crunchies."

The association of pirates with "treasure" remains for me to this day, making Jesus's repeated use of the word still sound odd. But disambiguating pirate treasure from heavenly treasure is a worthwhile endeavor. The theme of treasure/reward is central to Jesus's teaching throughout chapter 6, including 6:19-34.

Matthew 6:19-21 serves double duty in the skillful structure of the Sermon on the Mount. These verses are simultaneously the conclusion to the teaching of 6:1-18 and the introduction to 6:22-34. Matthew 6:19-21 is a hinge passage, a technique common in ancient rhetoric. In connection with 6:1-18 these verses are the concluding illustration of the exhortation and promise that motivated 6:1-18—we should not be so foolish as to live for perishable praise from other humans rather than the lasting reward with our Father in heaven. At the same time, 6:19-21 also transitions to Jesus's next topic regarding whole-person righteousness—our relationship to money and possessions.

Jesus's repeated point is again clear and strong: **disciples of Jesus must pursue wholeness.** As with responding to God's instructions (5:21-48) and in the practice of our spirituality (6:1-21), true life in God's kingdom will only be found in the way of "greater righteousness." This greater righteousness is not merely external but pays attention to our hearts, our inner person. Whatever we give our heart to is what we give our allegiance to, and therefore, our future (6:21). **There are few things in life that have more power to capture our allegiance than money and possessions**. Thus, in this next section of applying the principle of 5:20, Jesus turns to the goods of the world and the unhappy result of what happens when we live divided rather than wholehearted lives.

Coins minted by Pontius Pilate. ILLUSTRATOR PHOTO/BOB SCHATZ

God and Money
MATTHEW 6:22-24

Jesus's exhortation to **"store up for yourselves treasures in heaven"** (6:20) leads us into the theme of money and possessions and how these affect us. This will be applied with Jesus's pointed metaphor in 6:24—**"No one can serve two masters . . . You cannot serve both God and money."** But before He gets to this conclusion, He uses another image—the eye as the lamp of the body (6:22-23).

To modern readers, 6:22-23 seems to be a diversion from the topic of money into something else rather weird and confusing. By breaking these verses into their own paragraph, our editions of the Bible likewise indicate that these verses are disconnected from what comes before and after them. But 6:22-24 is one seamless argument. We only don't see this because we lack the cultural background to understand Jesus's metaphor of the eye as a lamp.

In the ancient world, many people described our ability to see as a function of light emitting from our eyes, like a modern-day flashlight. Thus, the eye is the lamp of the body in the sense that it shines forth what is inside our souls, our hearts, and our inner person. When our eye is "healthy" then this reveals whether our hearts are light/good or dark/evil. The key to understanding what Jesus is saying is paying attention to this Greek word, *haplous*. While "healthy" is not a bad translation, the more fundamental sense of this word is "singular" or "whole" (which is contrasted with "doubleness," as in James 1:8). If our eye is "whole" then this results in and shows that our inner person is light. Thus, we see again the repeated theme in the Sermon of the necessity of our wholeness, consistency, or integrity between the parts of who we are, both inside and out.

But it still may not be clear to us what this has to do with money. When *haplous* is used in the context of money (as in 6:19-21 and 6:24) it has the connotation of being generous. The "whole eye" is contrasted in 6:22-23 with the "evil eye" which in the ancient world communicated envy, greed, and malice. For example, in Deuteronomy 15:7-10, God's people are told not to be stingy toward one another, which in the Greek version uses the phrase "evil eye" (Deuteronomy 15:9). Proverbs 23:6 and 28:22 also describe a greedy or stingy person as having an evil eye. And closer to home, in Matthew 20:15 the ungodly vineyard workers are described as having an "evil eye" because they are jealous and envious of the rewards that others around them have received. Here in 6:22-23 Jesus is contrasting the person who is focused on money (the "evil eye" person) with the one who is free from this fool's errand (the "whole eye" person). Once again, this is because "where your treasure is, there your heart will be also" (6:21).

Thus 6:22-23 flows naturally from 6:19-21 as a continuation of the same theme of how disciples are to relate to money—**we must not give our hearts to the fleeting treasures and pleasures of the world because this is the way of double-minded darkness not whole-person righteousness** (5:20).

This understanding of 6:22-23 leads directly into 6:24 which provides an application of this truth to our lives. Because of the sharp contrast between light and dark, Jesus reminds His disciples that there is no neutral choice in our hearts. **"No one can serve two masters, since either he will hate one and love the other, or he will be devoted to one and despise the other. You cannot serve both God and money"** (6:24).

Money and possessions are not neutral or insignificant. The metaphor of a master or lord is not merely coincidental. Money and possessions have the power to demand our allegiance at the heart level. As created goods they are not inherently evil, but their power must not be trifled with or ignored, like a child playing with a cougar. Jesus regularly speaks of "the deceitfulness of riches" (Mark 4:19; Matthew 13:22), a phrase that should give us pause whenever we are lulled into thinking we are not controlled by the power of wealth and goods. And Paul reminds us that **"the love of money is a root of all kinds of evil, and by craving it, some have wandered away from the faith and pierced themselves with many griefs"** (1 Timothy 6:10).

Workplace Goals

Money and work are always connected in our modern minds. One comes from the other. For many the goal for your job is provide a living and keep you occupied sharing your talents meaningfully in the workplace. At the same time, Jesus cautioned that it cannot become your master. Put a check mark before the guidelines that you may need to adopt to help you find the right balance at work.

_____I will choose work that does not habitually hinder my opportunity to worship or serve God.

_____Salary requirements will not be the ultimate determining factor in my employment.

_____In addition to striving to do good work, I will leverage my work to spend time praying about people I serve, my coworkers, and employer.

_____I will carefully weigh day-to-day business decisions to make sure that they do not disrupt my walk with God.

_____ I will release the idol of excelling at my career.

_____I will be more satisfied with pursuing a calling than attaining a certain title or salary.

_____My behavior in the workplace will demonstrate consistent integrity.

_____I will embody my faith and share it with my coworkers.

_____I will pray about my work goals and submit them to God.

_____Overtime will not be a goal if it means I do not get to spend quality time with family and friends.

_____I will acknowledge that every rung I climb on a career ladder is foremost a blessing of God and grace.

_____If I lose my job, I will trust God to provide another in His timing.

_____I will generously leverage extra income to share with others or to support important ministry.

_____I will set appropriate boundaries on the time I devote to my work in order to give my family, church, and friends my best.

_____I will manage the money I earn well, not spending it frivolously or focused on myself, but wisely with a kingdom mindset.

God, Money, and Anxiety
MATTHEW 6:25-34

Jesus continues His exhortations concerning the power of money in our lives in 6:25-34 with a "therefore" (6:25). He has just argued that money and possessions have a great potential power over our lives and so we must be conscious and vigilant about how our relationship to money both reflects and affects our hearts.

He now draws out the big implication for our lives with an extended discussion of anxiety. Three times Jesus will tell us **"Don't worry"** (6:25,31,34). But it may not be immediately clear what the "therefore" connection is. Let's follow the logic of what He wants us to see.

The main exhortation is to not worry, to not be anxious. It is entirely natural as a human creature in a fallen world to experience anxiety. There are many things that might cause us anxiety, some real and some imagined. There are circumstances that cause us worry, such as when a child, friend, or parent is sick or in danger. There are biological, neurological, and psychological causes of anxiety. Those who have been traumatized by war or abuse often experience anxiety in their bodies in a way that is not merely in their minds nor easily resolved with just a thought. Jesus is not addressing all forms of anxiety here nor giving a flippant response to just "Stop it!" as if mere talk and command can solve all of our problems. **Anxiety is not a sin like adultery that can be simply prohibited.**

So what is Jesus is saying in exhorting us not to worry? He is talking specifically about the self-inflicted anxiety that we experience when we try to live a double-hearted life, serving both God and money (6:24). When we try to serve both God and wealth, this splits the soul and results in anxiety, not wholeness. As we noted above, wealth is particularly potent in the splitting of our devotion, of making us not whole (*teleios*, 5:48) as the story of the rich young ruler also reveals (19:16-22). This otherwise truly righteous man lacks wholeness (*teleios* again, 19:21) precisely because he has so much wealth. This is why Jesus declares that it is difficult for a rich person to enter the kingdom (19:23-24)—wealth is a king always battling for allegiance with God, the true and lasting King.

Jesus does not want us to live this not-greater-righteousness double life because it will result in loss in the future (6:19-20) and anxiety now. So how do we retrain our hearts and minds to not invest foolishly and experience anxiety?

Jesus is not encouraging a denial of reality, nor that we should ignore all human circumstances and only think about spiritual things. Rather, **He is inviting us to do some reflection, considering what really matters and how the world really works.** In the first instance, He asks us to ponder the fact that food, drink, and clothing are not really what life is about (6:25). He is not saying these things don't matter. Of course they do! We've already been instructed to ask God to provide our daily bread and protect us (6:11). Rather, we are being reminded that these important temporal and external matters are just that—**temporal and external**. We are more than our circumstances and our earthly life.

So Jesus reminds us what really matters and then gives a couple of memorable examples of how the world works. He invites us to ponder birds (6:26-27) and flowers (6:28-30). Birds do not have the security of agricultural plans and barn storage, yet they survive. They still eat. Flowers do not have spinning wheels and thread to make themselves fine clothing, yet they are still adorned. They are clothed with beauty.

How does this help us? Because the same heavenly Father who feeds the birds and clothes the flowers is attending to us even more. Humans, the only creatures made in God's own image, His children, are infinitely more valuable to Him than birds and flowers. So how much more will He provide for our anxious needs (6:26b,30b)?

When we forget this and live with non-Father-conscious anxiety we show our "little-faith-ness" (6:30b). Jesus is not condemning His disciples with these words, but inviting us to renew our minds in recalling that we are not merely "Gentiles," that is, those who do not know God. Rather, we are children of the heavenly Father who knows our needs and cares greatly (6:32).

Therefore, we need not live in anxiety (6:25,31,34) because this focuses our hearts on an imagined reality "tomorrow" rather than the true reality of "today" in relationship to our heavenly Father (6:34). Anxiety about money and the goods of this world splits our souls between now and an imagined future. Our hearts will be whole/complete when we live in the today, including all its troubles, rather than this imagined future. Our Father is present now to provide our "daily bread."

The threefold exhortation to not worry is the primary focus. But Jesus also provides a positive counterbalance of what we should do. We should **"seek first the kingdom of God and his righteousness"** (6:33). The ultimate solution to soul-splitting anxiety is to redirect our thoughts, affections, and energy toward someone, something, and somewhere else—God's kingdom and righteousness.

By this point in the Sermon (and in the Gospel of Matthew) both the kingdom of God and righteousness have become focal themes. Jesus's ministry is an invitation to turn away from earthly kingdoms and ways and turn to God, learning to inhabit the world in a manner that accords with His coming heavenly reign. "Repent, because the kingdom of heaven has come near" (4:17). This can be described as "greater righteousness" (5:20) and "practicing righteousness" (6:1), as bearing fruit that accords with faith in Jesus the King (3:8) and "fulfilling all righteousness" as Jesus models (3:15).

When we set our hearts, minds, and habits on our heavenly Father's provision as citizens of His coming kingdom, we will find His provision to be sufficient and satisfying (6:33). This does mean that things will always go our way or that we will never be in want. Quite the opposite, Jesus assures us that faithfulness and righteous living will often result in suffering and loss (5:10-12). But faith is seeking His kingdom and righteousness out of trust that therein lies "treasures in heaven, where neither moth nor rust destroys, and where thieves don't break in and steal" (6:20).

Door from church of the Nativity
ILLUSTRATOR PHOTO/ LOUISE KOHL SMITH

Tying together all of 6:19-34, out of Jesus's love for us, He invites us to the greater righteousness in our relationship to money and possessions. The invitation is for us to find true flourishing by realigning our hearts and allegiances to a singular dedication to God and His coming kingdom. **Anxiety about money and provisions is often a warning light that we are trying to serve two masters—this world and its goods and Christ and His kingdom.** This splitting results in anxiety, not the flourishing we long for.

A CLOSER LOOK

God as Our Heavenly Father

God was not referred to as "Father" very frequently in the Old Testament, but in the Second Temple period (roughly 515 BC–AD 70) this terminology became more common. Around the same time, the Roman Senate would sometimes confer the title *patres patriae* ("father of the country") upon their highest rulers. So in the time of Jesus—which lies at the intersection of the Jewish and Roman worlds—referring to the God of Israel as "Father" was not unprecedented or shocking.

However, referring to God as Father was more frequent for Jesus than His contemporary rabbis and became the characteristic way that Christians referred to God. This is certainly related to the importance of Jesus as the Son of God, whose divinity and mission is repeatedly described in relationship to the Father and the Spirit.

The Gospels refer to God as Father over 170 times, most frequently in John and secondly in Matthew (44 times). The largest concentration of references to God as Father in Matthew is found in the Sermon (17 times). In every instance but one, Jesus describes God to His disciples as "Father" even as Jesus relates to God as Father.

The combination of "Father" with "heaven" is particularly frequent and important for Matthew, repeatedly using the phrases, "the Father in heaven" (5:16,45; 6:1,9; 7:11,21; 10:32-33; 12:50; 16:17; 18:10,14,19) and "heavenly Father" (5:48; 6:14,26,32; 15:13; 18:35; 23:9). This is part of Matthew's larger theme of contrasting the heavenly realm with the earthly realm, God's ways with humanity's (see 6:19-21). This juxtaposition of God as Father who is in heaven simultaneously emphasizes God's transcendence and familiarity, both His power and His personal connection.

The Lord's Prayer (6:9-15), central to the Sermon, is fundamental in teaching Jesus's disciples that their identity is as children of the Father in heaven. The major function of this "Father" language in the Sermon is to give Jesus's disciples a clear and distinct identity as the true children of the God of Israel (as opposed to the unbelieving Pharisees).

No Worries

The Bible brims with reminders that we don't need to worry—probably because as human beings our natural inclination is to worry first and ask God later.

Read the verses below to discover why you should not worry about anything today.

Psalm 55:22: I don't have to worry that God will abandon me because He will never let the _____ be shaken.

Isaiah 41:10: I do not worry that I am strong enough to deal with my problems because God _____ me and _____ me.

Luke 1:37: I don't have to worry about finding a solution to what seems like an insurmountable problem because _____ is _____ with God.

Philippians 4:6: Instead of worry, I can _____with _____ and present my _____ to God.

Mark 13:11: I do not need to worry about saying the right things when facing persecution because the Holy Spirit will _____ me what to say.

1 Peter 5:7: I can hand over all my worries to God because He _____.

Psalm 23:4: I don't even have to worry about the darkest valley (death), because He is _____ me.

Isaiah 35:4: I can assure others they do not have to worry either because God will _____ them.

Scripture is a wonderful tool to use against the temptation to worry. Which of these verses do you need to commit to memory or post where you can see it and be reminded that you have nothing to worry about?

Personal Reflection

The topic of money is not an easy one to look at honestly in our lives. Whether we are financially well-off or not, money does have a power over all of our lives.

Reflect on this phrase, "The deceitfulness of riches," and perform an honest assessment of the ways you might be under the deceptive sway of wealth, possessions, and the false security they offer us.

Anxiety is natural but not life-giving. Identify an area of your life that is marked by anxiety and prayerfully reflect on God's promises of provision in that area. What would it look like to seek first God's kingdom in that area?

What are some wrong notions you might have about God that can be corrected through thinking of Him as your heavenly Father? Do you tend to think of God as personal but not transcendent or maybe exalted and powerful but not relational? Why?

Crown of Anemone, the "lilies of the field."
UNPLASH

5

THE RIGHT WAY TO JUDGE

MATTHEW 7:1-12

"Don't judge me!" has become a mantra for many people in our society. It is most often used when someone is aware that what they are doing is morally questionable, spoken with an air of defensiveness. Because Christian morals have been so pervasive in Western civilization and especially in America, many people who utter this phrase are reacting to real or perceived disagreements between their behavior and the teachings of Christianity.

Things get especially sticky when someone who says "Don't judge me" is aware of Jesus's teaching in the Sermon on the Mount. They may not actually know much about the Sermon but Matthew 7:1 is one of those sayings that has woven its way into people's general knowledge. Thus, when someone senses that a Christian is disagreeing with their behavior, the response is often that this "judging" Christian is hypocritical and not following Jesus Himself. "Didn't Jesus Himself say, 'Don't judge'?" is often the vehement response. "How dare you question my choices and my morality while claiming to be a Christian?"

It is certainly true that religious people, including Christians, are often judgmental, harsh, and hypocritical. Jesus's words here do challenge His own disciples in this regard. We'll come back to this later.

But using "Do not judge, so that you won't be judged" as a way to justify one's attitudes and behaviors when they clearly violate biblical morality is far from what Jesus is saying. And to be a hypocrite, according to Jesus, is something deeper and more challenging than being a person whose actions and words don't always match. By this stringent and humanly-impossible definition, everyone is a hypocrite every day and the notion becomes meaningless. (See the Closer Look on "Hypocrisy" later in this chapter.)

We need to think carefully about what Jesus is saying and what He's not. **What does it mean to "judge"? What is a hypocrite and how do we avoid being one?** And when we keep reading in Matthew 7 other questions arise—What are the holy things we're not supposed to throw before dogs and the pearls that are to be kept away from the pigs? And who in the world are the dogs and pigs Jesus is referring to?

As we have been seeing throughout our study in the Sermon, absolutely central to a good interpretation of any part of the Sermon is its place in the whole. We will benefit by reviewing the Sermon's careful structure. In 7:1-12 we have reached the final section of the main body of the Sermon (5:17–7:12). The introduction to the body (5:17-20) referred to "the Law and/or the Prophets" and this phrase is used again to mark the conclusion of this section (7:12).

The theme of the necessity of greater righteousness (5:20) ties together the entirety of the Sermon and continues in 7:1-12. The greater righteousness Jesus calls His disciples to is doing the will of God not only externally, with our behavior, but also internally, in our hearts. Matthew 7:1-12 is the conclusion to the third application of Jesus's exhortation toward greater righteousness. The first application concerned relationships with each other as instructed by the Torah (5:21-48). The second application focused on our acts of piety toward God (6:1-21). The third application of greater righteousness applies to our relationship to the goods and people of the world around us (6:19–7:12).

Previously in this study (6:19-34) we saw how Jesus exhorts us to be wise in how we think about our relationship to money and possessions. Now **Jesus invites us to the same kind of whole-person wisdom when we think about our relationships with other people** (7:1-6). Jesus concludes this section by reminding us again of our heavenly Father's care and provision for us (7:7-11), even as He did in 6:25-34.

All of this is clear and beautifully structured. At the same time, this does not make 7:1-12 easy to understand or apply. The question still remains what exactly Jesus means by telling us not to judge. And the saying about holy things, dogs, pearls, and pigs is widely recognized as the most confusing and unclear adage in the Sermon. Most frustrating for students of the Sermon, unlike the rest of these chapters, it is not immediately apparent how 7:1-12 is structured and flows together. At first reading, it appears to be almost a random collection of sayings thrown in at the end.

But there is a structure and consistency throughout these verses. It will be helpful to understand the rabbinic pattern called the *kelal uferat* ("the general and the particular"). The *kelal* is the heading that states the theme of the text. This is followed by some particular examples and then a concluding, summary statement.

This works out in 7:1-12 in this way:

- 7:1-2—the heading, on evaluating rightly
- 7:3-6—the first example, evaluating people rightly
- 7:7-11—the second example, evaluating God rightly
- 7:12—the concluding aphorism about living wisely

Following these clues, we'll explore our text in these four parts.

Evaluating Rightly
MATTHEW 7:1-2

The overall message of 7:1-2 is in many ways straightforward. Namely, God has made the world in such a way that people reap what they sow (see Galatians 6:7-9), both physically and relationally. For those who live judging and condemning others, sooner or later, this will be turned on them. This is a generalized proverb about living wisely in the world. **We must choose how to live in relation to others, and this will affect our experience of others and even of God.** If we have a condemning attitude toward others, this will be our experience of the world. If instead we have a welcoming and accepting attitude, this will be our experience. This should remind us of Jesus's Beatitude about the merciful being shown mercy (5:7) and the fifth petition of the Lord's Prayer about forgiving one another (6:12). The same logic is used in 6:14-15, the addendum to the Prayer that connects forgiving others with receiving forgiveness from God. This is the same proverbial wisdom in the concluding words of 7:12, that we should treat others as we would want to be treated. Indeed, as we treat others, so too we eventually will be treated.

But we must still ask the question, *What does Jesus mean by not judging? Is He saying that no one ever has a right to say some idea, behavior, or person is wrong?* In short, no. To understand this we need to think about this English word *judge* and also how 7:1-2 fits in with the rest of Scripture's teaching.

While "do not judge" is a fine translation of Jesus's words here, we have a bit of a problem with the English word *judge*. In English today *judge* (especially when used as a verb) has come to mean almost exclusively "condemn." "Don't judge me" communicates to the modern English ear, "Don't condemn my actions." But this is a more narrow and negative sense of the word. More broadly, *judge* has the more general sense of "evaluate, discern, separate, or decide." This is the role of a judge, one who listens, perceives, and decides what is just (notice the same root), and then dispenses justice. Justice served is deliverance, safety, and victory to the one who is in the right and condemnation to the one who is in the wrong. This discernment process is what it means to "judge" here.

Thus, a better translation of 7:1 is "Do not judge unfairly." Matthew 7:2 uses another metaphor to communicate the same idea—**measure things with a fair measure even as you would want for yourself**. The point is not that all evaluations of others and situations must be avoided, but rather that disciples must evaluate and discern properly and fairly. In all our interpersonal relationships, we should not judge in a way that we ourselves would not want to be judged—unfairly (7:12).

Biblical scholar R. T. France sums it up nicely: This text deals with the "down-to-earth issue of unfairly critical attitudes to others, which, combined with a naïve lack of self-criticism, threaten to disrupt a close-knit community such as that of Jesus's first disciples."[1] We can see the same point being made in James 2:12-13 and 4:11-12, which tie brothers and sisters judging each other to speaking evil against each other and judging the law itself and which emphasize that judgment without mercy will be measured to those who have not been merciful.

Once we understand that the issue is discerning fairly and graciously, not a prohibition of all evaluation, we can make sense of how 7:1-2 fits in with the rest of Scripture. Throughout the Bible God is calling His people to discern rightly what is true, good, and beautiful and to reject false gods, false ideas, and false teachers. **Being discerning requires that we evaluate what is right and wrong and not be naïve and foolishly tossed about by every idea** (Ephesians 4:14).

Jesus clearly doesn't reject discernment. Just a few verses later, the disciples are called upon to classify some people as pigs and dogs so as to avoid them. This is not ultimate condemnation, but it is a judging or discerning of right and wrong in people. The same is presupposed in 7:15-20, where disciples are warned to be discerning about who is a wolf and who is a sheep, despite initial appearances. We could explore many other instances throughout Matthew such as 10:11-15 and 18:15-20, where disciples need to wisely decide who is a true follower of Jesus and who is not. Scot McKnight summarizes the nuanced point of 7:1-2 well: Christians can pronounce "that is good" and "that is wrong" but not "you are condemned by God."[2]

Evaluating People Rightly
MATTHEW 7:3-6

With this key principle articulated, Jesus proceeds with two spaces where we can apply it to our lives. The first of these is in the day-to-day practice of interpersonal relationships. This is a place where we are easily tempted to judge others unfairly, including within the community of Christ's disciples. Jesus uses a memorable and even comical image of a person seeking to "help" a brother by removing a speck from their eye, completely oblivious to the sight-hindering plank of wood in their own (7:3-4). I can't help but think Jesus got a bit of a laugh when He produced this image. **The absurdity and audacity of the attempted blind-eyed eye surgery is meant to shock us into self-awareness.** How often do we think we see the problems (the specks) in other people's lives while ignoring our own specks and even more glaring problems? In doing so, we violate the principle of judging fairly and being measured by our own measure (7:1-2). Jesus rightly calls this hypocrisy (7:5).

So what do we do? Consistent with Jesus's teachings throughout the Sermon, he challenges us to do the inward look, to do heart-level probing. We must first take the beam of wood out of our own eye. This means looking more closely at our own lives, how they may not be consistent with who we say we are and with God's will. Further, we must not be content with a merely surface level self-evaluation, but ask whether our hearts reveal lust, bitterness, anger, duplicity, a vengeful spirit, seeking the praise of others, and a love of money—in short, all the things Jesus has been teaching in chapters 5 and 6.

Once we have done this work (and keep doing it), then and only then are we able to render a fair and honest judgment on someone else's life specks. We completely miss Jesus's point, however, if we take Him to mean that we need to look at ourselves so that we can get right back to judging others. Removing the beam of wood from our own eye is not a quick-fix preliminary on the way to self-righteous condemnation of others. It is meant as a wake-up call to the self-deception that is always creeping into our hearts.

I like to refer to Jesus's instructions in 7:3-5 as the **"mirrors before windows"** principle. When we encounter disturbances in our souls, things that are upsetting us, we tend to blame circumstances and people outside of ourselves, and sometimes that is accurate (in part). But before we focus our attention outside of our souls—as windows—we need to first use what is bothering us to look inward—as a mirror. When we do this mirror/beam of wood removal work, we often find that what we thought was a window/speck issue with someone else is either not as large as we thought, is more complicated than we originally perceived, or is not really an issue at all.

After these instructions, 7:6 seems to come out of the blue. Its meaning and its connection with the rest of the teaching is unclear. The first problem comes in figuring out what all these metaphors mean—dogs, that which is holy, pearls, and pigs. In Jesus's day, dogs and pigs were definitely terms of contempt, in Jewish and non-Jewish usage. Likewise, "that which is holy" and "pearls" are universally understood positively. Within Judaism, pearls often refers to valuable sayings or excellent thoughts and the holy things here are likely teachings or truths about God.

So what is Jesus saying? A very common interpretation of this mysterious saying applies these instructions to the "fencing of the table" of the eucharistic meal from unbelievers. In the early document called the *Didache*, Christians are instructed that they should not give the elements of the Lord's Supper to those who have not been baptized because that would be violating Matthew 7:6. This is a reasonable application of this saying, for sure. Other scholars have suggested, however, that there is an even closer application within Matthew.

If "dogs" and "pigs" refer to Gentiles, this text corresponds with 10:5-6 and its prohibition of taking the gospel to Gentiles until after the resurrection and the Great Commission (28:16-20). Maybe the clearest interpretation is to connect this with Jesus's instructions in 10:14. There the disciples are instructed to not waste time wrangling with or entrusting their message to those who refuse to accept it. They should shake the dust off their feet when they depart from such closed-eared people.

Regardless which reading of this puzzling saying is the best, we can still inquire as to how this verse fits in with 7:1-5. Though it may not be immediately apparent, there is a connection with the speck-beam-eye teaching of 7:3-5. Namely, 7:6 provides the balancing wisdom to the instruction of 7:3-5. If 7:3-5 emphasizes hesitancy and extra care in discerning the faults of others, 7:6 supplies the counterweight or ballast lest we become foolish and undiscerning. There is a symmetry of wisdom here. While disciples must always be careful in evaluating others, they should not become too lax or lose all critical faculties when it comes to sacred concerns. There are false teachers and false prophets that must be noted and avoided.

A CLOSER LOOK

Hypocrisy

Jesus's enemies in Matthew are primarily "the scribes and the Pharisees." They regularly conflict with Him and eventually decide to kill Him, setting in motion Jesus's arrest, crucifixion, and death (12:14). In several places, especially chapter 23, these opponents are repeatedly described as "hypocrites" (15:7; 23:13,15,23,25,27,29; see also 22:18 and 24:51). Even though they are not identified specifically as Pharisees in the Sermon, the hypocrites are the main people Jesus uses as examples of the opposite of what He is teaching (6:2,5,16; 7:5). While hypocrisy is a more general phenomenon than Pharisaism, the Pharisees are a clear example for Matthew.

Typically in English usage today, *hypocrisy* refers to someone who says one thing but does the opposite. In common parlance, a hypocrite is one who lives a double life, whose actions and words don't match, such as a politician taking bribes while running a campaign against corruption. Hypocrisy is a kind of doubleness, thus it is the opposite of wholeness (being *teleios*). But Jesus is using the word to communicate something deeper and more challenging. Hypocrisy in Matthew is a doubleness of heart compared with actions. It is living a genuinely good moral life on the outside (no secret sins being covered up) but with a heart that is dead and disconnected to God. In chapter 23, Jesus will picture this as white-washed tombs and cups that are clean on the outside but filthy within (23:25-28). This has been the theme throughout the Sermon—the necessity of singularity between our inner and outer persons. Hypocrisy becomes the key way to describe this deficiency.

Because true righteousness is whole-person virtuous living, for religious people the more likely serious danger is not blatant immorality but a skin-deep righteousness that looks good on the outside only. Here in 7:5 is the only place where Jesus calls His potential disciples hypocrites, warning them in the starkest terms that judging others harshly without doing one's own plank-removal work is a sign of not truly following him (see James 1:26; 3:9-12). This hypocrisy is yet another example of the Sermon's theme of wholeness. Righteousness requires consistency between one's inner person and one's outer actions. Discerning the state of another without first examining one's own heart is a dangerous and deadly business precisely because it is a kind of doubleness.

Evaluating God Rightly
MATTHEW 7:7-11

As we discussed above, the structure of 7:1-12 is not as easy to discern and fit together as in the earlier parts of the Sermon. The words of 7:7-11 are powerful and meaningful even apart from any structural observations. But there is also a connection to the rest of 7:1-12. We are called to judge rightly and wisely (7:1-2). This applies to not condemning others and judging ourselves properly by looking at our own eye planks. This also entails reconsidering who God is, judging Him rightly as a compassionate and generous Father.

There is also a close connection between 7:7-11 and 6:25-34. In both texts Jesus emphasizes God's fatherly nature and care. While this may seem to modern Christian readers like a familiar notion, this emphasis on God as Father was not the primary way that Jewish people thought of God. But Jesus makes this the central idea, and more than an idea, the central relational experience by which His disciples should approach God. (See Closer Look in the 6:19-34 study.)

So what is this Father God like? Using the analogy of a good human father, Jesus invites us to consider God in the same way:

> *"Who among you, if his son asks him for bread, will give him a stone? Or if he asks for a fish, will give him a snake? If you then, who are evil, know how to give good gifts to your children, how much more will your Father in heaven give good things to those who ask him."*
> **MATTHEW 7:9-11**

There is nothing more natural than for a father to joyfully provide for his children, especially when they ask. Using a "lesser to greater argument" (as He does in 6:25-34) Jesus reminds us that even human fathers, who are inconsistent and flawed (here described hyperbolically as "evil") know how to give good gifts. Since this is true, how much more lovingly and consistently will God the Father provide for our needs.

This encouraging vision for who God is for us is the basis for Jesus's memorable and poetic invitation in 7:7: **"Ask, and it will be given to you. Seek, and you will find. Knock, and the door will be opened to you."** Rather than being reluctant or unsure about approaching God, we are instructed to boldly ask, seek, and knock.

In line with 6:25-34 (including the parallel instruction to "seek first the kingdom and his righteousness" in 6:33), in all circumstances we are summoned to redirect our hearts upward to the powerful and compassionate Father "and all these things will be provided for you" (6:33). If we have lingering doubts about God's attitude toward us, Jesus makes it clear that we can pray to the Father in heaven. As Peter will later say it, turn with humility to God **"casting all your cares on him, because he cares about you"** (1 Peter 5:7). The emphasis is not on the skill or even persistence of the seeker in prayer (as in Luke 11:5-8; 18:1-8) but on the character of kindness of the heavenly Father.

Unlike our tendency to examine only outward appearances and then judge people unfairly, God by contrast is shown to be fully and wholeheartedly loving—He blesses all who look to Him. He is not reluctant to give and forgive, to bless and provide, knowing what we need even before we ask. James reflects on this same truth in telling us, **"Now if any of you lacks wisdom, he should ask God—who gives to all generously and ungrudgingly—and it will be given to him"** (James 1:5).

Elderly woman in a doorway of old Jerusalem.
ILLUSTRATOR PHOTO

They Asked, He Answered

The Bible records many instances when God answered the prayers of people who had the faith to turn to Him about their circumstances.

Read the verses to discover who the person was. Write down the essence of their prayer.

	Name	Request
Acts 12:5-16	_____	_____
		_____
2 Kings 20:1-5	_____	_____
		_____
Judges 16:28-30	_____	_____
		_____
Exodus 33:18	_____	_____
		_____
1 Samuel 1:10-11	_____	_____
		_____
James 5:17	_____	_____
		_____
2 Kings 6:17-20	_____	_____
		_____

Living Wisely
MATTHEW 7:12

The main body of Jesus's teachings in the Sermon conclude with 7:12, another one of Jesus's famous sayings from the Sermon: **"Therefore, whatever you want others to do for you, do also the same for them, for this is the Law and the Prophets."** This adage is so memorable and practical that it has for centuries been called the "Golden Rule." The simplest paraphrase of 7:12 is that disciples should treat others in love. Whether Christians are known for being loving or not, both those inside and outside the church recognize this is what Jesus taught.

As we noted when discussing 6:19-21, sometimes verses serve double duty. This is the case with 7:12 as well. It helpfully sums up the exhortation to evaluate each other fairly (7:1-11) while simultaneously concluding the theme of greater righteousness in relation to the world (6:19–7:11), and even more broadly, providing the right-hand bookend to the whole central section of the Sermon (5:17–7:12).

Jesus's words in 7:12 are not foreign to the Jewish tradition but stand in great continuity with the teachings of Israel. The "Golden Rule" can be understood as a pithy wisdom form of the second greatest commandment to love one's neighbor as oneself. This is the second part of the summary of the law ("Love God and love neighbor"), which is itself a summary of the two tablets of the Ten Commandments, as Jesus says in Matthew 22:34-40. The rabbi Hillel offered a comparable negative version: "What is hateful to you, do not do to your neighbor. That is the whole Torah, while the rest is commentary" (b. Šabbat 31a). The apostle Paul reiterates the same sentiments: **"For the whole law is fulfilled in one statement: Love your neighbor as yourself"** (Galatians 5:14) and "Do not owe anyone anything, except to love one another, for the one who loves another has fulfilled the law" (Romans 13:8).

Matthew 7:12 beautifully summarizes Jesus's way of being in the world that no amount of externally obeyed rules or regulations could ever encompass. The "Golden Rule" is not so much a rule but a vision (maybe better then, the "Golden Vision"). It is an invitation to the virtue of living in Jesus's way of love in relationship to others. Once again we are invited into the way of "greater righteousness" to fulfill the law and the prophets (5:17-20). The way of being whole (*teleios*, 5:48) is the way of wholehearted love.

Tying back into 7:1-2, we are reminded that no one wants to be judged unfairly or condemned. Therefore, it is hypocrisy to treat others this way. Jesus's way is the way of love, guided by this practical and universally applicable guide, "How would I want to be treated?"

Refining Gold

Applying the Golden Rule to life seems so simple because you set the standard.

Consider the value statements below and put a check mark beside ones that you agree with for how you want to be treated.

___ The first to get to a door should hold it open for others.

___ Cutting a line is never acceptable.

___ Drivers who make mistakes in traffic should hear about it.

___ Personal comments about one's appearance are taboo.

___ Criticism should be shared only in private conversations.

___ Praise should be shared with the entire group.

___ Humor is great but not at someone else's expense. Self-deprecating humor is the best.

___ Sharing a sincere compliment affirms.

___ Flattery does no one any good.

___ A failure to greet others or inquire about their well-being demonstrates indifference.

___ Honesty and candor are more important than privacy.

___ Hearing directly about a problem from the person directly involved is much better than learning about it secondhand.

___ Setting boundaries is perfectly fine.

___ It's okay to ask to borrow money or possessions.

___ No one in need should have to ask to borrow money or possessions because they have already been offered.

___ Being left out of a group outing may cause pain.

___ Forgiving mistakes or failure should be the norm.

___ Anyone who asks for forgiveness should automatically receive it.

___ Promoting someone's self-sufficiency or independence is just as important as offering a helping hand.

Did any of the statements give you pause? Read Proverbs 20:5 for deeper insight on why we should take the time to understand what's buried in the heart so we can treat others with the care we would want.

Personal Reflection

When you see something questionable in someone else's life, what is your first thought? Is it judgment?

Before letting these thoughts go any farther, pause and do some self-reflection. What beams of wood are in your own eye?

The particular issue may be different. The one you're judging likely struggles in an area you pride yourself in being good at.

But what areas do you struggle to live wholeheartedly and virtuously? Prayerfully spend time reflecting on this in humility before the Lord.

What areas in your life cause you anxiety? Accepting Jesus's invitation to ask, seek, and knock, take some time and cast these anxieties upon Him.

This is as simple as praying for God's provision, turning away from false hopes of trusting in earthly riches or people. This is seeking first His kingdom.

Do you believe God is a perfect and caring heavenly Father? Explain.

Sometimes we need to kick-start our hearts to remember this truth. Reflect on God's goodness, His provision in the past and in the present, and the confidence we can have in His future provision. Psalm 103 is a good place to kick-start our hearts into praise and thanksgiving. He is the Father who gladly gives good gifts to His children.

Read Psalm 103 and reflect on God's goodness to His children.

1. R. T. France, *The Gospel of Matthew*, The New International Commentary of the New Testament (Grand Rapids: Wm. B. Eerdmans, 2007), 273–274.
2. Scot McKnight, *Sermon on the Mount*, The Story of God Bible Commentary, edited by Tremper Longman III and Scot McKnight (Grand Rapids: Zondervan, 2013), 312

6

TWO WAYS OF LIVING

MATTHEW 7:13-8:1

A few years ago, I noticed some places on the side of my house where the bricks and the mortar were separating. Once I detected these disconcerting gaps, I found other places as well. These places on the exterior corresponded to small cracks in the drywall I had seen inside the house. I realized that due to some clogged gutters, water was getting near the foundation of the house and causing some unsettling settling. I was able to fix the problem before further damage was caused. But when the foundation of a house is weakened, damage and destruction follow. It is with this kind of vivid and memorable image (including this particular metaphor) that Jesus concludes His masterful message, the Sermon on the Mount.

The "mount" part of this sermon comes from the geographical references that frame the whole message. In 5:1-2 we read that when Jesus saw the crowds that were following Him, "He went up on the mountain, and after he sat down, his disciples came to him. Then he began to teach them." Following Jesus's deep and practical teachings, the response of the hearers is amazement at His clarity and authority (7:28-29). Then Matthew 8:1 provides the symmetrical mountain-referencing ending—"When he came down from the mountain, large crowds followed him."

This same intentionality of structure marks the inside of the Sermon, as we have seen. The final section of teaching (7:13-27) is no exception. In the introduction to the Sermon (5:3-16), Jesus casts a vision for true life that can be found in following His paradoxical ways. The emphasis is on true happiness or flourishing (*beatus; makarios*), following the lead of Psalm 1. Now in the conclusion, Jesus returns to this theme. He offers a comparable series of images that serve as warnings about missing God's will and kingdom. Like Psalm 1, the book of Proverbs, and many other wisdom teachings, Jesus paints a picture of two opposite ways of inhabiting the world. One will lead to life and one will result in loss and destruction.

The old Roman Road from Jerusalem to Jericho.
ILLUSTRATOR PHOTO/JAMES MCLEMORE

This is an appropriate and powerful way to wrap up His profound teachings about the greater righteousness that are found throughout the body of the Sermon (Matthew 5:17–7:12).

The conclusion to the Sermon consists of three subsections of teaching—7:13-14, 7:15-23, and 7:24-27. Each of these teachings use metaphors or parabolic images to invite us to feel the weight of Jesus's words. The broad and narrow paths, the true and false prophets, and the wise and foolish builders make clear that our response to Jesus cannot be neutral—it is a choice of one path or the other. Throughout this conclusion the same Sermon-wide theme of wholeness can be found.

Copying Psalm 1

Fill in the similar key words of Psalm 1 that Jesus also used or referenced in the Sermon on the Mount. You will find them in the word bank following the passage:

How _____ is the one who does not

walk in the advice of the wicked

or stand in the _____ way with sinners

or sit in the company of mockers!

Instead, his delight is in the Lord's instruction,

and he meditates on it day and night.

He is like a _____ planted beside flowing streams

that bears its _____ in its season,

and its leaf does not wither.

Whatever he does prospers.

The wicked are not like this;

instead, they are like chaff that the _____ blows away.

Therefore the wicked will not stand up in the judgment,

nor sinners in the assembly of the _____.

For the Lord watches over the way of the righteous,

but the way of the wicked leads to ruin.

WORD BANK

wind   fruit   righteous   happy   pathway   tree

The Broad and Narrow Paths
MATTHEW 7:13-14

In the first of the three parts of the conclusion, Jesus describes two different paths that a person can take. **One road is wide, smooth, and comfortable. The other is narrow and difficult.** Each road has a comparable entrance gate. Jesus says that the wide way is easy to traverse, so lots of people go that way. The narrow road must be sought after and few people find it. More than just describing this scenario, Jesus is instructing His disciples to go down one of the paths and not the other. The first word of 7:13 is a command—"Enter!"

The idea of two different paths is not odd. What is shocking is which path Jesus instructs His disciples to follow. One would think that the smooth way would be the better path, tapping into the idea that the way of the righteous is blessed by God with favor and success. Proverbs 4:18 tells us that **"the path of the righteous is like the light of dawn, shining brighter and brighter until midday"** and Isaiah was called to prepare the way of the Lord and make **"a straight highway for our God in the desert"** (Isaiah 40:3). But Jesus says that it is the rough road that leads to life while the broad way leads to destruction.

Herein lies the same unexpected and disruptive teaching that Jesus gave in His Beatitudes—the way of God's people will be marked by suffering and even persecution, but it is the way of reward with the Father in heaven (5:10-12). This is why Jesus calls the good path the narrow and difficult way. It is the "pressed down" way, the cramped and troubled way.

What is this seemingly unpleasant path that actually leads to eternal life? It is the way that Jesus has been describing throughout the Sermon— the greater righteousness that comes from doing the difficult work of looking inside our hearts and letting God do a deeper work there. It is becoming whole (5:48). The broad way is the way of external religion that the Pharisees and scribes model. This way is easy because it provides a set of rules and regulations that we can perform without ever doing the painful work of examining our motives and becoming people of love for others. While this way is easier now, it will result in destruction.

True and False Prophets
MATTHEW 7:15-23

Jesus's second of three concluding exhortations is the longest and most complex. **It weaves together two different metaphors—wolves that are dressed as sheep and trees bearing fruit.** The second of these images is a common one throughout the Sermon and all of the New Testament (see Closer Look below). The first image is less common but easily understandable. The complexity comes from the combination of these two different metaphors in a way that is not immediately clear.

The point of the wolves in sheep's clothing image is straightforward. Jesus warns His disciples to beware, that is, to be wise and discerning, because there will always be some people who appear as good on the outside but are evil on the inside (7:15). These false prophets may make bold claims and even appear to do miracles (7:22), even as the magicians in Pharaoh's court did in trying to mimic the power of God through Moses (Exodus 7:22). But such external actions are not the same thing as truly doing the will of the Father in heaven (Matthew 7:21) and truly knowing God (7:23). Merely proclaiming that Jesus is Lord without being connected to Him in the inner person is not sufficient (7:21). This is consistent with the whole message of the Sermon—**external religious behavior is good but is meaningless if it is not rooted in a true knowledge of God.** Jesus will repeat this same idea in the lamenting woes pronounced over the Pharisees in Matthew 23. These people appear to be sheep (and shepherds) but are actually self-serving wolves.

This is clear enough, so why does Jesus also illustrate this with the familiar tree and fruit metaphor? The point of the trees and fruit image is you can tell what kind of tree is in front of you and how healthy it is by what kind of fruit it produces. But if a false prophet/wolf is doing apparently good things and looks like a sheep, then it seems you can't always tell a tree by its fruit! When these two metaphors of wolves and trees are smashed up together, they appear to be saying the opposite thing. In the one case it's supposed to be obvious what kind of person someone is. In the other case, they have a disguise that makes them not appear to be who they are. How do these fit together?

Jesus is intentionally weaving these metaphors together to add more nuance to both of these truths. The point is that there are times when you can't immediately tell whether something is good or bad, whether it be an animal, a tree, or a person. Initially, even an unhealthy tree or a prophet may appear good. But sooner or later the true nature of someone and something will come out. A tree always eventually shows itself by its fruit. That "later" may be as late as Jesus's return when all people stand before Him as He righteously judges the whole world, separating the sheep from the goats (25:31-46), or it may be sooner. But all will be revealed—false prophets and sheep-costumed wolves will be shown to be as they really are. Their fruit will be examined by the Lord and shown as healthy or not, corresponding to their true tree-nature.

So Jesus is calling His disciples to beware and be wise. We shouldn't be quick to judge others or judge unfairly (7:1-5), but neither should we be naïve (7:6). When exercising discernment, we must value what Jesus values—not flashy miracles and prophetic abilities but a true and genuine heart. Sooner or later this will always come out.

Thistle in Jordan
ILLUSTRATOR PHOTO/TERRY EDDINGER

A CLOSER LOOK

Tree and Fruit

The Bible uses a lot of examples from human experience that are translated into profound spiritual truths. One of the most frequent of these is the agricultural image of a tree and its fruit. From Genesis to Revelation we find this metaphor used regularly. For example:

Genesis 1–2—The repeated command when God makes the world is that everything would "be fruitful and multiply" according to its kind.

Genesis 3—The whole tragic story of humanity's fall is connected to a tree whose fruit Adam and Eve ate in disobedience to God.

Psalm 1—The path of destruction versus the way of true life for all humans is described as the difference between chaff and being a fruit-bearing tree.

Matthew 3—John the Baptist warns the religious leaders of his day that although they have all the trappings of external holiness they need to repent. This repentance looks like "bearing fruit"—a change in their lives at the heart level.

John 15—On the last night of Jesus's earthly life He teaches His disciples that He is the True Vine and His disciples are the branches. If the branches remain connected to the vine, they can produce fruit, but if they do not, they will shrivel and die and be removed.

Galatians 5—The apostle Paul describes the difference between a Christian and non-Christian in terms of whether God's Spirit is dwelling in them. How can you tell if this spiritual rebirth has happened to a person? The lives of those without the Spirit manifest various sins (Galatians 5:19-21), but in the believer the Spirit brings forth beautiful fruit (5:22-26).

Revelation 22—The whole story of the Bible ends with the reversal of what happened back in Genesis 3. In the new creation there is a river of life and "the tree of life was on each side of the river, bearing twelve kinds of fruit, producing its fruit every month" (Revelation 22:2).

All of this provides the backdrop for Jesus using the same image in the Sermon. In the Sermon this metaphor is utilized to emphasize the importance of seeing us as whole people. The kind of tree we are will eventually manifest itself in a certain kind of fruit. As we follow Jesus, He transforms us on the inside so that our lives will increasingly bear spiritual fruit on the outside.

Date Palms
AILLUSTRATOR PHOTO/TERRY EDDINGER

The Wise and Foolish Builders
MATTHEW 7:24-27

The third and final image in Jesus's Sermon is appropriately climactic. Jesus describes two different people who build their houses in two different ways. One lays the foundation of his house on sand and the other on rock. The difference between these two people and their respective houses is described as wise versus foolish because sooner or later each house will undergo trial and stress. When it does, the wisdom or foolishness of the foundation work will be revealed. The rock-built house will be able to withstand the winds and water while the sandy foundation will give way, resulting in destruction of the whole house in dramatic fashion.

It's not difficult to discern Jesus's point from these contrasting images. Whether the winds and rain are referring to trials in life or the final judgment (I think it is both), the point is clear—how a person builds the house of his or her life matters. This is classic wisdom teaching as seen throughout the Bible. God regularly instructs His people to live wisely because of its benefits both now and in the age to come.

Likewise, throughout the whole Sermon, Jesus has been inviting people to live their lives based not on mere traditions but on divinely given wisdom. Jesus is the Great Teacher and Prophet who reveals the mysteries of the kingdom of heaven to those who have ears to hear (Matthew 13:10-17). He is the Authoritative One who must be listened to because He alone is the Son of God. As God's voice from heaven announced at Jesus's baptism, **"This is my beloved Son, with whom I am well-pleased"** (3:17).

This is the context for the shocking claim that Jesus makes in 7:24-27. The difference between the wise and foolish builders' foundations is not just general wisdom but is specifically focused on hearing and doing Jesus's words. If any reader has not picked up on the Jesus-centeredness of the Sermon yet, it should be clear now. Jesus is the exact representation of God on the earth who gives the final word (Hebrews 1:1-3) and therefore His words have greater authority than anything. He begins by authoritatively pronouncing what true happiness is (Matthew 5:3-12), how to rightly interpret Torah (5:17-48), what really matters in terms of piety (6:1-21), and who the Father in heaven is and how He cares for His people (6:19–7:12). We should not be surprised at this climactic conclusion to the Sermon, that the wise person is the one who listens to Jesus's words.

Jesus redefines the source of God's life-giving wisdom to be Himself. It is hearing and doing His teaching that creates wise people. This is what it means to be a disciple—to be a wholehearted follower of Jesus as Teacher and Model of the true wisdom from God.

Merely hearing Jesus's words is not enough, however. We must respond with a change of life or else we've not really heard. This response does not come from our own power nor does it earn our way into a covenant with God. The ability to understand Jesus comes from Jesus revealing the Father to us (11:25-27).

Our covenantal relationship with God comes through Jesus's sacrificial atoning death and resurrection that provides forgiveness for our many sins (26:26-28). But these things are not the opposite of the need for us to repent (3:2; 4:17) and produce fruit that is consistent with repentance (3:8). God's children are those who truly do the will of God (7:21; 12:50), who practice their righteousness in wholehearted ways (6:1).

This is why Jesus concludes the Sermon by reemphasizing that wisdom is seen in both hearing and doing what He teaches (see James 1:22-25; 2:14-26). Jesus redefines the source of this life-giving wisdom to be Himself. It is hearing and doing His teaching that creates wise people. This is what it means to be a disciple—to be a wholehearted follower of Jesus as teacher and model of the true wisdom from God.

Stones in the foundation of Herod's Temple Mount construction, each stone had a frame design with a rough center the frame was larger at the bottom than the top and most were wider on the right than the left. ILLUSTRATOR PHOTO/G.B. HOWELL

Wise Words

Fill in the blanks below to discover how the Bible defines wisdom:

Psalm 90:12: _____ us to number our days carefully so that we may develop wisdom in our _____.

Proverbs 1:7: The _____ of the LORD is the beginning of _____; fools despise wisdom and discipline.

Proverbs 2:6: For the LORD gives wisdom; from his _____ come knowledge and _____.

Proverbs 13:10: _____ leads to nothing but strife, but wisdom is gained by those who take _____.

Proverbs 11:12: Whoever shows _____ for his neighbor lacks sense, but a person with understanding keeps _____.

James 1:5: Now if any of you lacks wisdom, he should _____ God, who gives to all _____ and without criticizing, and it will be given to him.

James 3:17: But the wisdom from above is first _____, then _____, _____, _____, full of _____ and good _____, without _____.

Tying the Conclusion Together

The book of Psalms in the Old Testament begins with one of its most famous songs, Psalm 1. Psalm 1 is considered a "wisdom" psalm because of its description of the flourishing life ("Happy is the one . . . " in 1:1) which is described via two different paths one can take—either the way of the wicked or the life centered on God's revelation. The second Psalm focuses on the Messiah, God's anointed king on earth, who will confound and overthrow all those who foolishly oppose Him. These two psalms are intentionally tied together by using the same word—*happy/flourishing/blessed*—at the beginning and the end (1:1 and 2:12). This is a helpful frame for considering what Matthew wants us to understand about Jesus—He is the anointed King who is also the teacher of true wisdom.

The conclusion to the Sermon (7:13-27) is deeply connected with Psalm 1 on purpose to emphasize Jesus as the giver of wisdom. In many ways these verses are a retelling of Psalm 1 by the ultimate Son of David, with an added urgency because of the imminent kingdom of heaven coming to the earth. Both Psalm 1 and Matthew 7:13-27 invite hearers onto the path of wisdom (Psalm 1:1; Matthew 7:24), contrast two paths or ways of being in the world (Psalm 1:1,6; Matthew 7:13-14), use fruit bearing trees as a key metaphor (Psalm 1:3-4; Matthew 7:16-20), speak of final judgment and separation of the righteous from the wicked (Psalm 1:5-6; Matthew 7:13,21-23,26-27), contrast those whom the Lord "knows" and those He does not know (Psalm 1:6; Matthew 7:23), and emphasize hearing and heeding God's revelation (Psalm 1:2; Matthew 7:24).

At the same time, the conclusion ties back into the entirety of the Sermon. The theme of wholeness that was used throughout the body of the Sermon (5:17–7:12) is what ties off the triad of teachings in 7:13-27:

- **7:13-14**—The difference between the way that leads to life and the way that leads to destruction is not found in the appearance of which ways looks better. Quite the opposite, the broad and easy path is the way of externally focused religious practice, while the narrow and difficult road is Jesus's way—the way of greater righteousness that will often result in persecution.

- **7:15-23**—The difference between true and false prophets is the inside of the person, not merely the outside. False prophets are wolves, even if for a while they appear as sheep. Their true internal nature will eventually be manifested. Therefore, we should value wholeness.
- **7:24-27**—The difference between the wisely and foolishly built houses is not the appearance of the house itself, but the hidden, interior foundation that will only be revealed in times of trouble and judgment. A beautiful looking house that is built on sand will not stand, while even the shabbiest place that is built on the solid rock will last.

Consistent across all three examples is Jesus's emphasis on true happiness (5:3-12) coming only through greater righteousness (5:17-20), or to use our more common language—**true life is found in Jesus when we live wholehearted lives.**

The Response of the Crowd
MATTHEW 7:28–8:1

As we noted above, Jesus's teachings are followed by Matthew the narrator coming back in and telling us how the people responded to His words:

> *When Jesus had finished saying these things, the crowds were astonished at his teaching, because he was teaching them like one who had authority, and not like their scribes.*
> **MATTHEW 7:28-29**

If you keep reading in Matthew you will see that this positive reaction will not always be the people's response to Jesus. Opposition to Him will increase, especially among the religious leaders (see 12:14). But for now, most people are happily shocked by His words because He taught with such clarity. This was quite unlike what they were used to from the scribes, who would offer complicated, detailed explanations of various rabbinical views on this topic or that. By contrast, Jesus speaks right to the heart and with practical and accessible images, explaining who God is as our heavenly Father and how He wants us to find life through living in His ways. People rightly sensed that Jesus had authority. In the following chapters Matthew will show us that Jesus's authority is not only in teaching but also over demons, sickness, nature, and even the ability to forgive sins (8:27; 9:6; 11:27; 26:64; 28:18).

As a result of this authority, when Jesus came down from the mountain, Matthew tells us "large crowds followed him" (8:1). This is a good word for us two thousand years later. Jesus is also calling us to follow Him. The Sermon on the Mount is not the entirety of Jesus's teachings, even in Matthew, let alone the other Gospels. Nor is the Sermon on the Mount all that we need to know to understand the Christian faith. But Jesus's teachings in the Sermon are a good place to start and to continually return to as we seek first God's kingdom and His righteousness and build our lives with wisdom upon the rock of Jesus.

Sea of Galilee from the Church of the Beatitudes. ILLUSTRATOR PHOTO/BOB SCHATZ

Personal Reflections

Do you expect your life to feel like a broad path and easy road? Jesus's exhortation to enter into the kingdom by the narrow gate is a reminder that the godly life will not always feel good circumstantially.

Are there areas of your life where you are resentful to God because of the suffering and difficulty you are experiencing? It's okay to be honest and lament before the Lord. But Jesus also wants us to recalibrate our expectations—following Him is not always easy.

The teaching about false prophets and their claims to be doing good things can feel rather scary. Were these people self-deceived and if so, could that be true of me? Some disciples of Jesus may hear Jesus's words and become paralyzed in fear that this may be true of them. But Jesus's words here are not meant to cause disciples to live in fear and crippling self-doubt that they may actually be wolves in sheep's clothing. Anyone who is willing to look inside and repent is no wolf. Jesus is challenging us to value whole-person righteousness, not just outward appearance and gifts.

Are there ways in which you might be overvaluing external gifts in yourself or in others rather than a heart that is attuned to God?

As we come to the conclusion of Jesus's most famous message, this is a good time to do an honest assessment of our hearts. Take some quite time to slow down and look inside in candid sincerity before your heavenly Father.

Identify two or three areas of your life where things may look good on the outside but you know there is deeper work for God to do in your heart.

Maybe it's in anger, careless use of words, judging other people, practicing piety to be seen by others, or the ever-present lure of money and possessions. Jesus has not come into the world and into our lives to condemn us but so that we can find the wisdom and flourishing life we are made for. This will only happen as we become more whole, so don't hold back but submit in honest humility before Him. "Blessed are the poor in spirit, for the kingdom of heaven is theirs" (5:3).

What is your biggest takeaway from this study?

ABOUT THE AUTHORS

Jonathan T. Pennington wrote the Personal Study Guide. He is currently Professor of New Testament Interpretation at Southern Seminary in Louisville, Kentucky. He is also the Spiritual Formation Pastor at Sojourn East and regularly speaks and teaches in churches all over the country.

He earned a BA in history as well as a teaching certificate from Northern Illinois University. He received the master of divinity degree from Trinity Evangelical Divinity School (Chicago), where he also taught Greek for two years as a NT Fellow.

He holds the PhD in New Testament studies from the University of St. Andrews, Scotland (in St. Mary's College), where he wrote a thesis entitled "Heaven and Earth in the Gospel of Matthew" under the supervision of Professors Richard Bauckham and Philip Esler. He has published a wide variety of books, articles, and Greek and Hebrew language tools.

Kima Jude wrote the Activities for this Personal Study Guide. She is a member of The Oaks Baptist Church in Grand Prairie, Texas, where she leads the women's ministry and her husband Barry serves as pastor. Kima has a bachelor's degree in journalism from Marshall University and had an early career as a newspaper reporter followed by a freelance writing career. She has written for several Christian publications, including Lifeway's *January Bible Study* and several *Explore the Bible* group plans.

She is employed full-time at a local university in the Dallas-Fort Worth region directing foundation relations and writing proposals. She and her husband are the parents of four young adult children and three young grandchildren. She looks forward to helping them discover the wonder of the Bible.

ALSO AVAILABLE

An item related to teaching this Personal Study Guide is the *Sermon on the Mount: Blessings of the Kingdom* (January Bible Study 2024) *Leader Guide* (item number: 005842157). The Leader Guide includes commentary, teaching plans, and a redeemable code for a digital download with additional helps.